**Learn and Play the Green Way**

# LEARN and PLAY

## the Green Way

FUN ACTIVITIES
WITH REUSABLE MATERIALS

**Rhoda Redleaf**

**Redleaf Press**®
www.redleafpress.org
800-423-8309

Published by Redleaf Press
10 Yorkton Court
St. Paul, MN 55117
www.redleafpress.org

© 2009 by Rhoda Redleaf

Originally published in 1999 as *Learn and Play the Recycle Way: Homemade Toys That Teach* by Rhoda Redleaf and Audrey Robertson

Second edition 2009
Cover design by Soulo
Interior typeset in Arno Pro and designed by Percolator
Interior photos/illustrations by City Desktop Productions
Printed in the United States of America

**Redleaf Press Editorial, Design, and Production Staff**
Editor-in-Chief: David Heath
Managing Editors: Laurie Herrmann and Douglas Schmitz
Acquisitions/Development Editor: Kyra Ostendorf
Creative Director: Jim Handrigan
Production Editor: Laura Maki
Production Assistant: Carla Valadez

15 14 13 12 11 10 09 08     1 2 3 4 5 6 7 8

FSC

**Recycled**
Supporting responsible
use of forest resources

Cert no. SW-COC-002283
www.fsc.org
© 1996 Forest Stewardship Council

Library of Congress Cataloging-in-Publication Data
Redleaf, Rhoda.
     Learn and play the green way : fun activities with reusable materials / Rhoda Redleaf.
          p. cm. — (Learn and play the green way)
     Includes index.
     ISBN 978-1-933653-70-9
     1. Toy making. 2. Educational toys. 3. Recycling (Waste, etc.) I. Title.
TT174.R4 2008
745.592—dc22                                                                2008026705

Printed on 100 percent postconsumer waste paper

# Contents

# Acknowledgments

The wealth of homemade ideas in this book and its predecessors, *Teachables from Trashables* I and II and *Learn and Play the Recycle Way,* is a tribute to the creativity and energy of the wonderful child care teachers, family child care providers, trainers, and others who make up the Minnesota child care community. Many of these ideas have been developed and shared over the years in classes, workshops, and conferences at Resources for Child Caring and elsewhere. I want to acknowledge and thank the many past and present staff members, trainers, and caregivers who have indirectly contributed to this book. Some of the ideas may have morphed considerably as they have been adapted to reflect present day knowledge, but many of the original, classic features remain.

I also wish to thank those who have been directly involved in the production of this book. Megan Davis did a beautiful job rewriting and adapting much of the text into the present format. It was a pleasure working with Kyra Ostendorf, the developmental editor who meticulously looked over endless details and wrote the "Green Ideas." As always, the production team did a magnificent job putting it all together. Thank you also to David Heath, editor-in-chief, and Linda Hein, publisher, for making this all possible. Thank you all for your outstanding work.

This latest edition celebrates a remarkable thirty-year history for Redleaf Press, since *Teachables from Trashables* was the first book published by then Toys 'n Things Press in 1979. This nostalgic trip down memory lane has made me acutely aware of the immortality of words and ideas and the mortality of those who create them. I cannot help but remember fondly all the years of working with Audrey Robertson, the creator of most of the infant and toddler ideas in this book and my coauthor of its immediate predecessor *Learn and Play the Recycle Way,* who died of cancer in 2007. I know she would be thrilled that all of our work those many years ago lives on in this latest edition.

# Introduction

## A LOOK AT LEARNING

Much has been written in recent years about the importance of learning in early childhood. The trend pushing for earlier and earlier academic learning is one result of this attention. In response, the National Association for the Education of Young Children (NAEYC) has revised its position statement for developmentally appropriate practice in working with young children. This position emphasizes the importance of planning opportunities to foster learning. Young children learn through direct, hands-on manipulation of their environment and a great deal of repetition. They learn best if they are at play and the learning emerges as a by-product of that play. You can enhance the learning environment by asking questions, making associations between the known and unknown, and stimulating interest and curiosity through the toy selection and activities offered. You don't, however, need a constant flow of new toys. Often, reorganizing or adding to familiar toys and activities reawakens a child's interest in them.

The items described in this book are intended to be used in play—and in that sense they are toys. But these items also provide stimulation for major developmental and learning processes. The many skills that are involved in this growth and development process are often grouped into the following six broad areas:

**Physical and motor development skills** are learned through the body and include large (gross) and small (fine) muscle movement.

**Sensory perception development skills** use the five senses, alone or in combination, and are crucial in learning to recognize and distinguish everything around us.

**Social and emotional development skills** deal with feelings, getting along with other people, understanding oneself and one's community, and being able to help oneself.

**Cognitive development skills** are those learned through the mind and include all the "thinking" skills, such as reasoning, problem solving, understanding basic concepts, organizing processes, math, and science.

**Language and communication development skills** include communicating without words, such as a baby's smile or a toddler's point. These skills also deal with verbal language skills and prereading skills.

**Approaches to learning development skills** add the dimension of some intangible elements of "spirit" or aesthetics to the cognitive and sensory processes that are involved in imagination, artistic or dramatic appreciation, and dramatic expression.

All of these skills are referred to frequently throughout *Learn and Play the Green Way* in the "What They Learn" section of each activity.

Most toys included in this book serve multiple purposes, and you can use them in many different ways. This book suggests a few ways, and you and the children will discover many more. Feel free to exchange or substitute activities among toys of similar types. A few general suggestions may help you in maximizing some of the learning potential:

**Understand that repetition is a necessary part of learning.** Activities that may quickly bore adults often continue to interest children. Many of the toys and games may strike you as versions of "the same old thing." To children, however, each one is a new experience—and it is the children's enjoyment that is the most important consideration.

**Vary the difficulty** of matching games. Make discrimination tasks more complex or very simple to match the ability levels of the children involved in the activity.

**Capitalize on the interests of the children.** For example, a child who has no interest in matching games but who loves dinosaurs will often participate willingly if the matches are of different types of dinosaurs. A child's attention span grows directly in relation to his or her interest in the activity.

**Present one skill or task at a time.** Many matching games in this book include multiple matching criteria. This makes the game more versatile in the long run, but initially it allows you to emphasize one criterion (for example, color). Generally, older children will show interest in the more complicated multiple-criteria tasks.

**Recognize the literacy value of cue cards.** These cards not only serve as clues while playing a game but also introduce the concept of symbols representing meaning, a prereading skill.

**Realize that children's learning about games with rules is a slowly evolving process.** Young children frequently agree to rules but have no idea how to follow them and are not at all interested in the process. Avoid too many rules or "real games" that feature winners and losers.

**Adapt the toys in this book by incorporating elements of various cultures.** For example, you can include words from other languages in some of the board games and counting or matching activities.

This book was written to help people who care for children understand and enjoy the learning potential inherent in play. In addition, you may find this book useful for working with and including families in your curriculum, training new child care providers, training students or staff, and creating or augmenting your toy supply. Cherish the creativity and imaginative playfulness of childhood and appreciate its value for adults as well.

## HOW TO USE THIS BOOK

The different toys and activities included in this book are grouped into six age-related sections that range from infants to schoolagers. Sections one through five follow an age-related continuum from infants through schoolagers and allow for considerable overlap. In general, the more versatile and flexible the item is, the broader its age-related appeal. Section four is the only section to target a single age group, preschoolers (children three through five years old). The activities in this section focus on specific cognitive skills that are developing during the preschool years. The last section includes items that can be used with all ages. The age-related suggestions for the activities need not be taken as absolutes. As you work with each child on a daily basis, you will best be able to ascertain each child's developmental readiness, interests, and experiences, all of which will greatly influence how and when an activity will be useful for a particular child.

In addition to the "What They Learn" section, each toy includes these sections:

"About the Toy" describes the toy and ways children of different ages might use it. The suggested uses are just the beginning. Use your own creativity and encourage the children to use theirs to expand on the many possible uses of these items.

"Extending the Learning" describes ways to enhance the child's learning through informal, observation-based methods and often includes participating with the children.

"What You Need" offers a list of the materials needed to create the toy.

"How to Make It" gives you step-by-step directions for making the toy. In some cases, alternative materials, variation games, or related activities are included.

"Green Idea" provides ideas to expand the activity and connect with taking care of our Earth.

## HELPFUL HINTS FOR MAKING YOUR OWN TOYS

Once you have chosen a toy to make, carefully read through the "What You Need" and "How to Make It" sections. Note any safety considerations, particularly if infants or toddlers will be using the finished product (use safer substitute materials if you prefer). Generally, you'll find that the suggested tools and materials are readily available. The following are suggestions for selecting and using materials for toy making.

**All-purpose white glue** is usually marked *nontoxic* and, if so, is good for toy making. Many other glues contain substances that could be harmful if swallowed or inhaled, so be sure to check labels. Choose a brand that is marked *nontoxic*. Glue sticks are generally nontoxic and are handy to use for many projects.

**Felt-tip markers** add color and are easy to use, but they do have limitations. Permanent markers are usually toxic and should be avoided. Water-based markers are usually safe, but toys made with them should be covered with clear contact paper to avoid bleeding should they become wet. When making infant or toddler toys, use contact paper cut into shapes instead of markers.

**Contact paper** is used in toy construction to allow for easy cleaning and may increase the life of the toy. Brightly colored contact paper also helps attract a child's attention to the toy. Usually found in a variety of hardware or general retail stores, contact paper is a good investment for any serious toy maker. Patterned contact papers can be used in the same way as wrapping paper (see below). If the object or toy is flat, lamination is an alternative way to protect and preserve it.

How to use contact paper:

1. Measure and cut the amount needed. Lay the piece flat on a table with the adhesive covering side up.

2. Twist the edges to loosen the covering.

3. Carefully peel away the covering and leave the contact paper on the table with the sticky side up.

4. Lay items to be covered facedown on the contact paper. If needed, place a second piece of contact paper on top of the game pieces, sticky side down.

5. Smooth by rubbing the items with your fingers, then cut out the pieces. For single-side coverage, fold the edges over the sides of the game piece or artwork.

**Coding dots** come in all sizes and colors and are generally available in office supply stores. They usually come in boxes of 1,000 dots per color, so find other people who would like to share materials. Some craft shops and teacher-supply stores have mixed colors of dots or labels, and some office supply stores sell individual sheets or smaller packages.

**Wrapping paper** is useful for making puzzles and many kinds of matching games. Use new or used wrapping paper and look for attractive papers with six to eight or more repeating picture items. Use paper with an overall scene (such as a playground or a forest) or papers designed with all different kinds of items (such as trucks, rocket ships, animals, or flowers) repeated many times.

**Plastic containers and lids** of all sizes and shapes can be used for making and storing games. Cover cut plastic edges with heavy tape to create a smooth, safe edge on the plastic.

**Juice can lids** work especially well in many toddler toys or matching games. Use only the smooth-edge lids that come from pull-tab containers (popular on frozen juice cans). Glue pictures to the lids or use them in play as anything from play money to pancakes. Let the children invent uses for them too.

**Empty tape rolls** can be used as wheels, in a ring-toss game, or in other imaginative ways.

**Stickers and seals** can be converted into matching or board games by using assorted stickers, such as ones with a holiday or animal theme. Look for at least six different versions of the same category (for example, six pumpkins or six butterflies). Look for books of stickers in teacher-supply stores, instrument and sheet music stores, party shops, and drugstores. (Stickers found in party shops or drugstores usually cost more, so make sure the packages contain more than one sheet of each sticker.)

**Magnetic tape** is helpful to use when making toys. One side of magnetic tape is adhesive, like regular tape, and the other side is magnetic. This tape is generally available in hobby shops, craft shops, and hardware stores. Remember that magnetic products can damage computers; therefore, magnets of any kind must be kept far away from them. When cutting magnetic tape, it is important that the pieces are large enough that they cannot be easily swallowed by children.

**Velcro** is a self-gripping material that is a marvelous addition to toy making. Small pieces of Velcro added to matching games allow the parts to be matched without slipping and sliding out of place. Children can then carry the completed game around to show an adult. They can remove the Velcroed game pieces when they stop working or no longer want to play. Just remember that the "smooth" or "loop" part must be on one side of the toy and the "teeth" or "hook" part must be on the other for the Velcro to work.

**Tagboard** can be found in many office-, art-, or teacher-supply stores. Recyclable alternatives that work equally well are used file folders, backs of tab-lets or coloring books, shirt or stocking inserts, cereal boxes, or any other type of lightweight cardboard.

## FINDING MATERIALS FOR TOY MAKING

Discount stores, craft stores, outlet shops, hardware stores, fabric stores, and home-decorating stores are all good sources for materials to use in toy making. Ask the managers of these stores to save surplus or unsalable items for you. Families and friends are other good sources for securing large amounts of common household items or recyclable materials. Surplus from friends, families, and stores is a good source for some items, but browsing and sorting through the supplies requires time and careful looking.

## SAFETY CONSIDERATIONS IN MAKING AND USING TOYS

Always consider the safety needs of children when you make toys. Safe toys for children pass the following tests:

**They are clean.** Thoroughly wash and rinse all materials and containers before use.

**They have no sharp parts.** Tape or round off corners. Take special care in removing lids from metal cans to be sure they are smooth along the rim. (You can often accomplish this by running the can opener around the can several times.) Sand and oil all material that might splinter.

**They are too big to swallow.** For infants, toddlers, or any children who put nonfood items in their mouths, the general rule is that an object be—at the very least—1 by 1½ inches in size. If you must use small objects, tie a few of them together to make them bigger. When using sponges or sponge-like materials in infant and toddler projects, cover the items with sheer panty hose to prevent children from biting off pieces and choking on them. Do not use staples in toys you are making for infants and toddlers. If toddlers will be handling the toys you create, sewing or taping is much safer.

**They are made of nontoxic materials.** Do not use any material that could be harmful if touched, eaten, chewed, or smelled. Read the package instructions to make sure that markers, paints, and glue or other adhesives are nontoxic and safe for children (and adults) to use.

*Note:* Although the instructions for the toys in this book have been written with "kid-proofed" tests in mind, no one can guarantee the absolute safety of these toys or activities. Use care and common sense to make all toys as safe as possible. Most of the toys described in this book are intended to be made by adults for children to use. Constructing the toys frequently requires the use of sharp tools, such as scissors and knives, which are not safe for children to use. If the children help you make the toys, be careful about possible hazards and supervise the children while they are handling the tools. Do not leave sharp tools lying around where children can get to them if you are called away during the construction process. Never leave any type of plastic bag or other flimsy kind of plastic within the reach of young children.

# Infants, Toddlers, and Preschoolers

# Sensory Floor Pad

## Who

Nonmobile infants

## About the Toy

The pad serves as a safe place for nonmobile infants by creating a clear boundary that older children can learn to recognize and respect. The pad encourages nonmobile infants to safely explore a variety of materials by touching, smelling, tasting, listening to, and looking at them. Be sure to customize the infant's learning experiences to meet his stage of sensory development. For example, if the infant appears to be exploring by putting everything in his mouth, make sure the items on the pad are large, safe, and clean. To help an infant concentrate on the items on the pad, place him away from other children's activities, facing the items you set on the pad.

## What They Learn

Physical and motor development skills: At two months, most infants can raise their heads and chins up from the floor, making the Sensory Floor Pad an ideal learning toy. Between three and six months, infants will begin batting at, reaching for, and grasping objects within their line of sight. You can encourage this development by saying to an infant, "Reach for the rattle," or "Come get the fuzzy ball."

## Extending the Learning

Infants' physical development progresses in a relatively predictable order. As you watch an infant's development over time, notice that he begins by swiping at objects on the pad and by about four months can grasp and squeeze the objects between his fingers and palm. When an infant appears to have lost interest in an object, add another that has different qualities. Pay attention to which types of items seem to excite the infant and which ones seem to calm him.

## What You Need

- [ ] nonallergenic, twin-size mattress pad
- [ ] scissors
- [ ] wide seam-binding tape or iron-on hemming tape
- [ ] needle and thread or iron
- [ ] ruler
- [ ] Velcro
- [ ] glue
- [ ] sensory objects with interesting surfaces and sounds (such as colorful plastic lids, rattles, plastic scouring pads, large pom-poms, furry material, sturdy play animals, or other toys)

## How to Make It

1. Fold the mattress pad in half and cut it along the fold to create two sensory pads. You may want to leave the pad intact and use the folded section for extra padding.

2. Sew seam-binding tape all around (or use iron-on tape) to cover any raw edges.

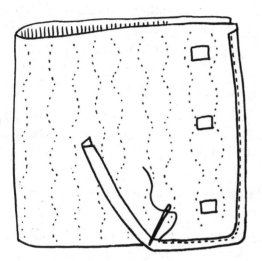

3. Cut three or more 1-inch pieces of Velcro. Glue or sew the soft sides of the Velcro to the top of the mattress pad at strategic locations. For example, three in a row (about 6 to 8 inches apart) on one, two, three, or all four sides of the pad.

4. Cut three or more 8-inch pieces of seam-binding tape. Sew or glue the remaining rough-sided pieces of Velcro to one end of each length of seam-binding tape.

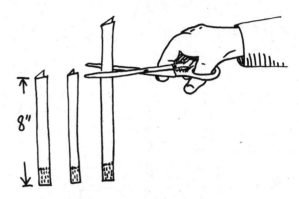

5. Tie or glue one sensory object to the other end of each length of seam-binding tape.

Take a toy inventory—throw away anything with chipped or flaking paint.

# Hanging Mobiles

## Who

Infants

## About the Toy

The mobile's bright objects and points of light attract the infant's attention almost immediately. Be sure to create and hang the mobile with the infant's point of view in mind, making sure the broad surfaces of the hanging objects can be seen. Ensure that all hanging items are securely fastened by giving them a good shake or tug before introducing the mobile to an infant.

**!** **Caution:** If you have other children who may try to investigate the mobile, hang it away from objects the children can climb, such as tables, chairs, and windowsills.

## What They Learn

Sensory perception development skills: Infants' perceptual abilities are much more advanced than once was assumed. The region of the brain that controls vision is very sensitive to stimulation and input from the environment. Since infants are most attracted to bold, bright colors and contrasting patterns, select objects for the mobile that include these attributes.

## Extending the Learning

One way to nurture sensory development in infants is to provide multiple opportunities for early sensory stimulation. Overstimulation (too many sights and sounds), however, actually works against healthy brain development in infants. As you observe an infant watching a hanging mobile, be sure she appears calm, content, and focused on the toy. Any signs of agitation, such as turning her head away from the mobile frequently, may signal it's time to change her activity or environment.

## What You Need

- ☐ aluminum pie tin
- ☐ juice can
- ☐ hammer and nail
- ☐ button
- ☐ yarn, string, fishing line, wire, cord, or shoelaces of various materials
- ☐ scissors
- ☐ colorful household objects (such as craft feathers, plastic or cloth fruit and vegetables, plastic

utensils, balls, pictures and designs from old greeting cards or magazines mounted on cardboard, empty spools, and small plastic bottles). Use only nontoxic objects and objects that are too large to choke on.

## How to Make It

1. With a hammer and nail, punch four small holes along the rim of the pie tin (equal distance from one another) and one hole in the middle. (Place the area to be punched over the open end of an empty juice can.)

2. Flatten any rough edges of the holes with the hammer. To hang the mobile, first thread yarn through the holes in the button and tie a knot in the end to keep the yarn from slipping through. Thread the yarn through the middle hole of the tin and make a loop at the other end.

3. Tie yarn to each of the four remaining holes in the tin. Hang objects from the yarn. Make sure the objects balance each other. You can hang any item by itself or in whatever balanced combination you feel will interest the infant.

## Variation

A single aluminum pie tin with multiple holes punched on its surface makes a neat light reflector when hung vertically by a sunny window.

Create a list of items that can be saved from the recycling bin and ask families to bring in the items so they can be reused in new ways with the children.

GREEN IDEA · GREEN IDEA

# Kick Toys for Infants

## Who

Infants

## About the Toy

Use elastic to attach this stuffed toy to the side railings of a crib, within kicking range of the infant. The infant is attracted to the toy by its facial features and bright colors. Kicking at the toy encourages muscle development and an awareness of cause and effect.

As soon as the infant shows signs of moving around in the crib, remove the elastic from the toy and the crib so that it becomes a cuddly toy for him. As a cuddle toy, it provides the infant with comfort through the sense of touch and a sense of security from being a familiar object.

The variations (see below) engage the child's awareness of sounds and movement.

## What They Learn

Cognitive development skills: In his studies of human cognitive development, Jean Piaget refers to the stage from birth to two years as the sensorimotor stage. During this developmental stage, an infant's behavior begins to shift from behavior controlled mostly by his reflexes to behavior that he controls purposefully, that is, behavior that is more goal-oriented. So although his kicks at the toy may be random at first, after a while he sees that the toy moves because he is kicking it—a milestone in his cognitive development.

## Extending the Learning

Infants grow so rapidly and acquire so many new motor skills, it's almost as if they become new people with each passing week. You may discover that the infant's random kicks at the cuddly toy fairly quickly turn into purposeful movements toward the fascinating toy dangling in front of him. Therefore, it's important to notice when he outgrows toys so that you can either make adjustments to the toy or remove it altogether, substituting for it others that are safe and appropriate for his new developmental stage.

## What You Need

- [ ] sturdy elastic (2 inches wide)
- [ ] ruler
- [ ] scissors
- [ ] Velcro
- [ ] two pieces of felt or other washable material (about 12 by 12 inches)
- [ ] small amount of contrasting material
- [ ] needle and thread
- [ ] nontoxic paint
- [ ] quilt batting

## How to Make It

1. Cut a 3-foot length of elastic. Attach three sections of Velcro across the middle of the elastic strip, approximately 3½ inches apart. Attach the elastic to the side railings of a crib or other convenient play space for infants.

2. To make the kick toy, cut out two circles of the felt or other material, each about 1 foot in diameter. For the facial features, use nontoxic paint or cut out facial features from the contrasting material and sew them securely to one of the felt circles.

3. Add Velcro to the back of the other circle 3½ inches apart (to match the Velcro on the elastic strip).

4. Sew the circles together, leaving a 3-inch opening. Stuff with quilt batting or other material until fluffy. Sew closed.

## Variations

Attach noisemaking objects to the kick toy, such as rattles, small wind chimes, or bells, by securely fastening them to a short length of seam-binding tape. Secure a small piece of Velcro to the other end of the seam-binding tape and attach this end to the elastic.

For added visual interest, attach different objects to a short length of seam-binding tape, as described above. Consider blocks covered with colorful Mylar-type bags from potato chips, small aluminum potpie pans, or other colorful kitchen objects, such as all-rubber spatulas.

Cut fabric in an area away from the children to prevent fibers from entering the breathing space.

GREEN IDEA · GREEN IDEA ·

# Infant/Toddler Activity Books

## Who

Infants and toddlers

## About the Toy

These tactile books are a fun and safe introduction to books for infants and toddlers. Create the books with the child's interests and developmental stage in mind. For example, since immobile infants are most interested in learning the characteristics of materials, the best type of book for them is one that includes a variety of sensory materials, such as colorful fabric pieces with different textures (including crinkly, smooth, rough, and squishy). Toddlers, on the other hand, love to explore and experiment. Pages with pockets containing small surprises, such as colorful bangle bracelets, clean keys that are no longer used, and large key rings, will entertain them and satisfy their natural curiosity. Be sure all items you use are nontoxic, washable, and too large for an infant to choke on or swallow—a minimum of 1½ inches in diameter.

## What They Learn

Sensory perception development skills: Infants quickly develop the ability to process and interpret information using their five senses. The sense of touch, in particular, is critical from birth. A caregiver's touch has a positive effect on the infant's emotions and health. In addition, infants use touch to learn about and interpret the world around them.

Through touching and exploring the characteristics of various objects, toddlers demonstrate their growing ability to think about objects around them and experiment with cause and effect.

## Extending the Learning

Initially, allow both infants and toddlers to explore the books in any way they choose. Doing so helps them begin to conceptualize the notion that books contain interesting information that satisfies their needs. As infant and toddler interest in the textures and objects grows, sit with them on your lap and discuss the textured materials and contents of the pockets with them. In doing so, you help to enhance their receptive and expressive language.

## What You Need

- ☐ one piece of fabric for the cover (about 7 by 15 inches)
- ☐ nontoxic, washable fabric paint (optional)
- ☐ five pieces of heavyweight pellon (about 6 by 14 inches) plus some extra for the pockets

- ☐ ruler
- ☐ scissors
- ☐ fabric glue, needle and thread, or sewing machine
- ☐ variety of textured fabrics and other materials (such as netting or scrubbing pads)
- ☐ small objects
- ☐ rickrack, shoelaces, yarn, or cording

## How to Make It

1. Decorate the front cover, if desired, with fabric paint or bits of fabric.

2. On a work surface, lay the cover material face down. Center one of the pellon pieces on top. Fold the excess ½ inch of cover fabric over the pellon and around the edges, mitering corners. Glue or sew in place.

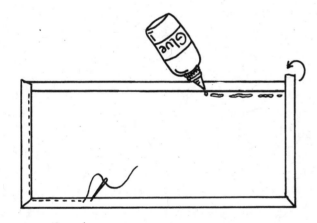

3. For pages that do not contain a pocket, glue or sew page contents, as desired, on four pieces

(eight pages) of pellon. Center the item on the inside of the cover. Sew or glue each page down the center. Fold in half.

## Variation

For toddler books, fashion different kinds of pockets. Sew or glue the pockets in place, one on each page. Cut pieces of rickrack a little longer than each pocket. Sew the ends of rickrack to the bottom inside of each pocket. Tie or sew the other end to an object, such as keys, key rings, or plastic lids. Hide the object in its pocket.

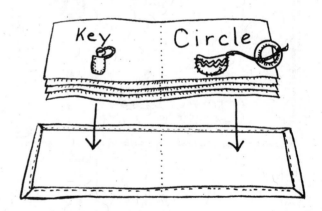

Invite older children to help make the books. Talk about the importance of reusing materials that would otherwise be thrown away.

# Cause-and-Effect Match Board

## Who

Infants and toddlers

## About the Toy

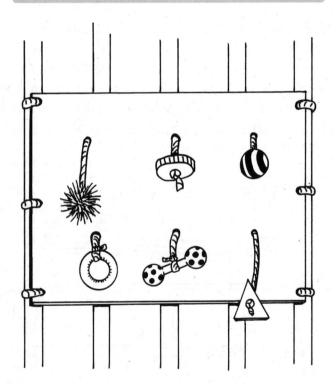

The bright colors and different designs on the match board encourage infants to use their eyes. At first, infants may be most interested in exploring the objects visually, and will progress to grasping and mouthing them. When an older infant discovers that pulling on an object on the board causes another object to move, the toy begins to appeal to her interest in movement and change. Using this toy helps infants and toddlers become aware of shapes, colors, and likenesses, and it helps develop hand-eye coordination and small-motor skills as the children discover, grasp, and pull. For toddlers, the toy helps develop hand-eye coordination and small-muscle skills as they discover what happens when they grasp and pull the objects.

## What They Learn

Approaches to learning development skills: The cause-and-effect action of the toy is interesting to infants and toddlers alike, and encourages them to take part in making change happen. You can share in a child's delight of discovery and movement by joining the child in side-by-side play on the board. By asking her questions about the different objects and how they move, you help satisfy her curiosity and her need to understand all of the amazing things around her. For example, you might ask, "What happens when I pull on this rattle? Oops! I make the squishy ball move! I want to do that again. Oops! There goes the squishy ball!"

## Extending the Learning

After a child has played with the board a few times, you may notice that some objects command her attention more than others. What characteristics of the objects are most appealing? Is she curious about their color? Shape? Texture? This is information you can use when selecting new objects for the board or when choosing other toys for her to play with, since the more she manipulates an object, the more she learns.

## What You Need

- [ ] heavy cardboard (8 by 11 inches)
- [ ] contact paper
- [ ] scissors
- [ ] X-Acto knife
- [ ] sturdy string or cord
- [ ] pliers
- [ ] nail
- [ ] assorted items (such as plastic lids; small, colorful containers; bracelets; rattles; curlers; pom-poms; spools; safe items from games with missing parts; film canisters; well-cleaned small plastic face cream containers; kitty treat containers; or toy animals)

## How to Make It

1. Cover one side of the cardboard with plain colored contact paper.

2. To hang the board, use an X-Acto knife to cut three small holes on each end of the cardboard. Thread a 12-inch length of string through each pair of holes.

3. Cut six more holes in the cardboard.

4. Cut three pieces of string: two pieces should be 16 inches long, one should be 20 inches long. Lace each string through two holes. (Lace the longest string through holes at opposite ends of the board.)

5. Choose three pairs of small plastic objects. Use a heated nail to make holes in each item (use the pliers to hold the nail while you heat it).

6. Tie the objects to the ends of each string.

7. Tie the board securely to a crib or other area where a child will have easy, safe access to it.

Be sure all the materials are safe for infants to handle and mouth.

# Pull-and-Snap Toy

## Who

Infants and toddlers

## About the Toy

A toddler reaches inside the can, finds the object at the end of the elastic, grasps it, and pulls it. When the child lets go, surprise! The object pops back into the can. The surprising action is much like a reverse jack-in-the-box and encourages the child to further explore the object in the can.

## What They Learn

Physical and motor development skills: By about six or seven months of age, an infant is able to pull strings to obtain an object as well as grasp the object with his hand. Here, both infants and toddlers are refining their small-muscle skills and practicing hand-eye coordination by repeatedly pulling and letting go of the object in the can. By repeating this process, they also learn to predict and expect a certain outcome from their own actions. A toddler might also discover he can remove the lid the object is connected to, which then becomes another action he will practice over and over.

## Extending the Learning

Knowing the progression of physical and motor development in children takes the guesswork out of selecting toys that are appropriate for them. However, even if you lack a solid understanding of the physical and motor stages of children's development, children will usually give you signs that indicate whether or not they are engaged and attentive. If you notice him looking away, turning his head, or becoming fidgety, that could be an indication that the toy you have chosen is still a bit too advanced for him.

## What You Need

- [ ] can with a plastic lid
- [ ] can opener
- [ ] contact paper
- [ ] wide elastic
- [ ] scissors
- [ ] needle and thread
- [ ] graspable object

## How to Make It

1. Remove the metal ends from a can. Use a can opener to make sure the ends are completely smooth.

2. Cover the can with contact paper, making the contact paper about 1 inch longer than the can at each end. Fold the excess amount over and into the inside of the can. Be sure there are no sharp edges.

3. Cut a piece of elastic the same length as the can. Then, in the middle of the plastic lid, cut two slits large enough for the elastic to go through.

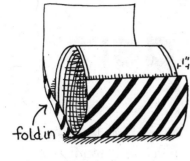

fold in

4. From the inside of the lid, lace one end of the elastic through the slits, and sew securely.

5. Securely fasten the other end of the elastic to the graspable object (such as a pom-pom, a small animal, or a soft ball).

6. Place the lid on the can so the object and elastic are inside the can.

Dispose of the ends of the cans with your other recycling.

# Box Blocks, Climbers, and Sliders

## Who

Older infants and toddlers

## About the Toy

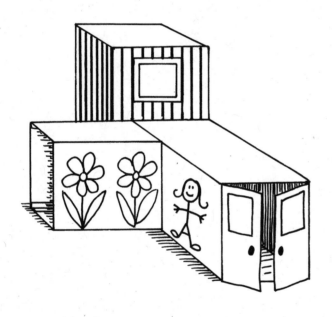

Using this set of basic blocks hooked together as a simple space divider for older infants provides them with a safe, confined area that also allows them to see and be seen. This way, they still feel as if they are a part of the group and yet remain secure behind a box enclosure. Tailor the boxes to the children. Choose boxes that are the best height for the infants to use for pulling themselves up (gross-motor activity), and choose boxes with a flat surface for playing with small toys (fine-motor activity).

Blocks made in a variety of shapes and sizes provide active toddlers with endless opportunities to climb over, through, and around, slide down, and so on. When weight is added to boxes, toddlers are encouraged to work together to push, pull, and lift them into place. In the block area, the boxes can be a fun addition to the other building toys.

## What They Learn

Physical and motor development skills: Once infants are able to sit without support, their next physical task is to pull themselves up to stand. By tailoring the height of the boxes to an infant and providing a safe space for practicing, you encourage this exciting new stage of development. For toddlers, boxes structured and arranged as climbers and sliders help them continue to practice a variety of gross-motor skills. In addition, toddlers build muscle strength and kinesthetic awareness.

## Extending the Learning

Children learn through play, and as they grow, they pass through different stages of play. Toddlers who use the boxes for building and constructing are engaged in constructive play. Constructive play involves manipulating objects with the goal of creating something new or imagined. It can also involve putting objects such as large boxes together to make representations of things in the real world. When children construct in this way, they expand their ideas of the world around them as well as create new ideas.

## What You Need

☐ large, sturdy cardboard boxes in various shapes

☐ newspaper

☐ duct tape or packing tape

☐ utility knife

☐ ruler

☐ pencil

## How to Make It

1. Select boxes to suit your needs. Large, flat boxes can be used to make platforms. A number of boxes that are all the same size and shape are ideal for using as building blocks or creating portable barriers. Large, sturdy boxes are great for making tunnels, and large rectangular boxes can be made into slides.

2. To weight the boxes, invite the children to crumple the newspapers and tightly stuff them into the boxes. Tape the boxes shut.

3. To make a crawl-through tunnel, use two boxes equal in size. Force one of the boxes several inches inside the other. Cut two holes large enough for toddlers to crawl through, one each on opposite sides. As an option, place a sit-upon in the bottom of the box (see p. 80).

4. To make a slide, securely tape all ends of a large box and cut as shown. Stuff the bottom part with newspapers. Turn the top part around and reposition it over the bottom to create the slide. For the two pieces to fit together, it may be necessary to bend down the bottom ramp. Securely tape the two sections together.

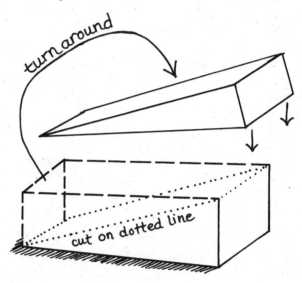

turn around

cut on dotted line

## Variations

Invite the children to decorate the boxes with markers or paint, or place Velcro on the boxes to help hook them together when desired, such as for a climber/slide combination or a train.

When the children are finished with the boxes, break down the cardboard and recycle it.

GREEN IDEA · GREEN IDEA ·

# Lid Box

## Who

Older infants and toddlers

## About the Toy

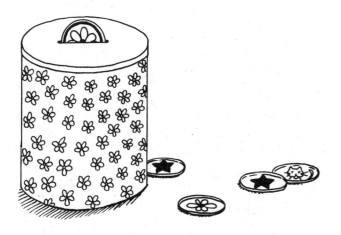

This toy provides great practice in filling and dumping, a favorite activity of older infants and toddlers because of their fascination with objects disappearing and reappearing. For older infants, remove the plastic lid and let them dump out the metal lids, or replace the lid on the can and let them drop the metal lids through the slot, one at a time. Infants and younger toddlers will enjoy the noise the metal lids make. Create several sets of cans and lids so toddlers can each have one as they play side by side.

## What They Learn

Cognitive development skills: Filling-and-dumping activities help children experiment with the concept of object permanence, one of two basic competencies children work to acquire during the sensorimotor stage of cognitive development. Object permanence involves knowing that objects continue to exist even when they are out of sight. The first hint of object permanence understanding usually emerges around four to eight months.

## Extending the Learning

How do you know a child understands an object exists even though it can't be seen? Children who grasp the concept of object permanence begin actively searching for hidden objects—that is, they know the objects are out there somewhere, and they're going to find them!

## What You Need

- ☐ large can with a plastic lid
- ☐ can opener
- ☐ contact paper
- ☐ scissors or X-Acto knife
- ☐ small pictures or fabric samples
- ☐ glue
- ☐ metal lids from juice cans

## How to Make It

1. Use the can opener around the top of the can until the rim is smooth. Cover the can with contact paper, making the contact paper about 1 inch longer at each end than the can. Fold the excess amount over and into the inside of the can. Be sure there are no sharp edges.

2. In the plastic lid, cut a slot about ½ inch wide and 2 to 3 inches long. (Use a metal lid as a guide for correct length.)

3. Cut out simple pictures or samples of different textured fabrics and glue them onto the recessed side of the juice can lids. For matching activities, make two of each picture or texture.

Old tennis ball cans work great for this activity.

# Poke and Peek

## Who

Older toddlers

## About the Toy

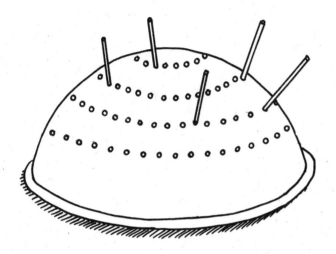

This Poke and Peek can be used for a group of two to four older toddlers. Children can enjoy playing next to each other without having to take turns or wait. Give each child an envelope with ten thin drinking straws or plastic coffee stirrers. Invert the colander and encourage the children to poke the straws all the way through the holes. When all of the straws have been poked through the colander, lift it up, redistribute the straws, and the fun begins all over again. This is also an absorbing activity for a toddler playing on her own.

**!** **Caution:** Be sure to remind toddlers that the straws are only for poking into the colander, never at other children.

## What They Learn

Physical and motor development skills: As a toddler works to poke straws through the holes in the colander, she is perfecting her fine-motor skills—skills that involve finely tuned movements with the fingers as well as hand-eye coordination. Other fine-motor activities that are appropriate for older toddlers include picking up small food items such as raisins, putting objects into a container, scribbling with large crayons on large pieces of paper, and stacking small blocks.

## Extending the Learning

Gross-motor skills involve the large muscles in arms and legs, and fine-motor skills involve the small muscles in fingers and hands. As you observe a toddler trying to fit the straws through the holes in the colander, note how successful she is with the task. Does she struggle and need assistance at first? With practice, she will learn how to manipulate smaller and smaller objects. Fine-motor activities such as this one also pave the way for basic self-help skills she will need as she grows; skills such as buttoning and unbuttoning her sweater or zipping and unzipping her coat.

## What You Need

☐ colander or a large clump of playdough

☐ thin plastic drinking straws (cut in half) or plastic coffee stirrers

☐ envelopes or other small containers

☐ scissors

## How to Make It

1. Place ten to fifteen straws into each envelope or small container. Store the envelopes or containers in the colander for easy access.

2. Give each child one envelope or container of straws. Invert the colander and let the children poke their straws through the holes.

## Variation

Let the children poke the straws into clumps of soft playdough.

When the children are finished, wash the straws and use them again for another sensory experience or craft project.

GREEN IDEA · GREEN IDEA

# Parasheet

## Who

Older infants, toddlers, and preschoolers

## About the Toy

The parasheet helps infants and toddlers become comfortable with brief separations from trusted adults and experience space differently. Make the parasheet the appropriate size for the number of children (and adults) in the group—two, three, or up to fifteen. To introduce the parasheet to infants and toddlers, first have them sit around it, helping to lift or simply watching the adults lift the edges and wave it gently up and down. After children become familiar with the parasheet, they will enjoy discovering new ways to use it, such as crawling under it, anticipating its up and down motions, using it to play peek-a-boo with familiar adults, and bouncing to the rhythm of verses or music that accompany the activity. It provides practice with the concept of object permanence, as in peek-a-boo. This fascinates older infants and young toddlers who are learning that objects that disappear will also reappear. It gives toddlers and younger preschoolers an opportunity to act upon a different material, and to experience the results of their actions. Older preschoolers will experience the concept of catapulting or launching an object into the air using the parachute as a tool.

Talking about real uses for parachutes develops vocabulary and enhances language development. Counting the times the children can keep a toy bouncing on the parachute provides practice in using numbers.

## What They Learn

Social and emotional development skills: The child-development studies of Erik Erikson explain how children develop socially and emotionally. His theories involve the notion that at each stage of a child's social and emotional development, specific tasks must be accomplished—ones that establish the foundation for more difficult tasks as the child grows. According to Erikson, during the first year of life, a child's task is to develop a sense of trust in himself, in others, and in the world around him. By using the parasheet to play games of peek-a-boo, adults can help build that important foundation of trust by demonstrating that although things disappear, they reappear just as quickly. These games help infants and toddlers become more comfortable with brief separations from trusted adults.

## Extending the Learning

When you first introduce peek-a-boo games with infants, do they seem unsure about whether the adult hiding beneath the sheet will ever reappear? This is normal. After a while, however, you will begin to see a shift from apprehension to delight when their favorite person pops back up from behind the sheet with a big smile on her face. Listen for the giggles and belly laughs—sure signs the infant is well on his way to trusting his world.

## What You Need

- ☐ an old flat bedsheet
- ☐ ruler
- ☐ chalk
- ☐ scissors
- ☐ sewing machine or iron-on hemming tape
- ☐ colorful scraps of material or iron-on designs for decorating (optional)
- ☐ small objects to use with the parachute

## How to Make It

1. Fold the bedsheet into a square (measure the shortest side, then measure off an equal distance on the long sides). King- or queen-size sheets are good to use with large groups; half of a twin-size sheet will work for groups of two to four participants. Cut off any excess material.

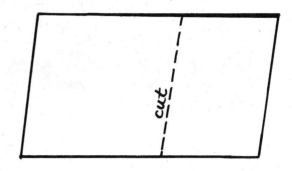

2. Fold the remaining square in half, then in half again. Measure the length from the center corner along the folded edge to the end. Using this distance, mark with chalk every few inches to create a semicircle line from edge to edge. Cut along the chalk marks.

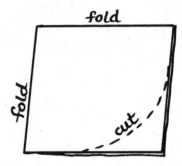

3. Create a hem. Decorate as desired.

## Variation

Sew small bells inside cloth patches and attach them to the top of the parachute to add an auditory element to this activity. If using bells, be sure they are securely attached and covered to prevent infants or toddlers from accidentally choking on them.

Save the scraps of fabric for the art center or another toy.

# Super Crawl-Over Box

## Who

Infants, toddlers, and preschoolers

## About the Toy

This box provides a safe way for infants to experiment with new crawling skills, learn to coordinate different large-motor skills, and enjoy the satisfaction of mastering a new skill. For infants, place the box on the floor for them to experiment with new crawling skills. They will enjoy crawling over it or pushing it along the floor. Toddlers may lift and carry the box around, balance on it, jump off it, or find their own creative uses for it.

## What They Learn

Physical and motor development skills: Between twelve and eighteen months, a toddler experiments with more difficult gross-motor skills, such as balancing on both feet, balancing on one foot, stepping on and off, and climbing and jumping. The Super Crawl-Over Box allows her to practice all of these skills, and to feel a real sense of accomplishment when she masters something new.

## Extending the Learning

While observing the many ways a toddler uses the box, you can encourage further experimentation and also help develop her expanding language skills. For example, comment on what she is doing and ask her open-ended questions: "Wow! You just took a big leap off the box! How far did you jump? What will you do next? See if you can jump even farther? Okay, show me how far you can jump this time. I'm watching!"

## What You Need

☐ sturdy cardboard box (about 3 by 12 by 18 inches)

☐ newspaper

☐ heavy tape

## How to Make It

1. Tightly stuff the box with crumpled newspaper.

2. Tape the box shut.

## Variations

Attach rope handles to one or two sides for easy dragging or lifting.

Make Milk-Carton Blocks (see p. 204), and tape them together before covering with contact paper to make crawl-over boxes of different sizes and shapes.

Make small stairs for advanced crawlers and toddlers. Create stairs by taping two shallow boxes together, the smaller one centered on the larger one, to create a 6-inch-wide step on all sides. Use sturdy, well-stuffed boxes. Tape them closed before covering them.

When the children are finished with the box, take it apart and recycle the newspaper and the cardboard.

GREEN IDEA · GREEN IDEA

# Push-It/Sort-It

## Who

Infants, toddlers, and preschoolers

## About the Toy

These soft and colorful textured blocks and shapes are perfect for an infant's need to touch and visually explore things. Toddlers will be challenged by pushing the shapes through the hole in the lid, then dumping them out. They may also enjoy gathering and dumping the shapes into or out of purses or other containers. Older toddlers and preschoolers might discover the soft shapes are perfect for practicing their throwing skills, which at first involves the use of both hands. Throwing the shapes may progress to games of catch with you or with another child and to taking aim at targets you set up, such as boxes or laundry baskets. Also consider adding the soft blocks to any existing block collections as new building materials for children to use.

## What They Learn

Cognitive development skills: Because of the many learning opportunities inherent in block play, block areas are standard features in early childhood classrooms. Some of the cognitive skills and concepts children are working on when they play with blocks include understanding size, weight, and height; using problem-solving skills related to building structures; and counting and categorizing.

## Extending the Learning

Depending on the age of the child, the Push-It/Sort-It toy will be used in different ways. An infant will focus on examining the blocks through his sense of touch, sight, and taste, whereas a toddler or preschooler will focus more on what he can do with the blocks, such as fitting them through the hole in the lid, throwing them, and constructing with them. Observing a child's preferred activities will enable you to guide his play in directions that are appropriate for his level of development.

## What You Need

- [ ] nonflammable foam rubber (about 2 inches thick)
- [ ] serrated knife
- [ ] a variety of textured fabrics
- [ ] needle and thread
- [ ] colorful socks or clean panty hose
- [ ] large tin can and several plastic lids
- [ ] colorful contact paper
- [ ] scissors
- [ ] pencil
- [ ] tracing paper

## How to Make It

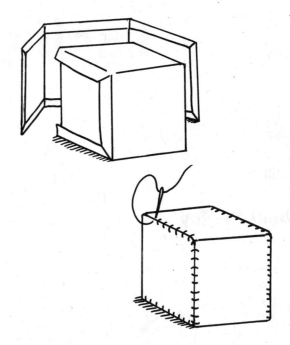

1. For foam rubber cubes and shapes, use the serrated knife to cut the foam rubber into 2-inch cubes (or different sizes and shapes).

2. Trace the following pattern on paper and cut it out. Use the pattern to cut designs from selected fabrics.

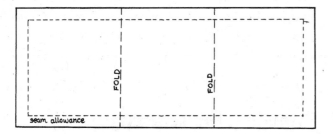

3. Cover the foam rubber with fabric (such as corduroy, velveteen, fake fur, or satin) and stitch the seams, or slip the foam rubber cube into a section cut from a sock or panty hose. Make sure the section of sock or panty hose is long enough to allow for tying off each end with strong thread.

4. Cover the tin can with the contact paper. In the middle of the lid, cut out a square or cut out holes shaped to match selected foam rubber shapes. The greater the child's dexterity, the smaller the holes can be. For the very young and inexperienced child, make the holes somewhat larger than the objects.

> Used sponges that have been sterilized can be used in place of the foam.

# Lacing Things

## Who

Toddlers

## About the Toy

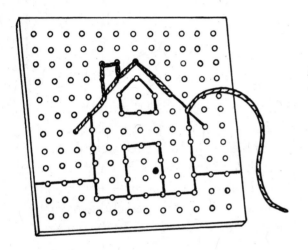

These sturdy lacing boards will last much longer than cardboard sewing cards. Lacing activities encourage hand-eye coordination, small-motor development, and problem-solving skills. To help an older toddler begin lacing, pull the lace through one hole near the picture's corner and demonstrate poking the lace through the holes along the outline, going back and forth from the front to the back of the board. Younger toddlers may lace in a random fashion and not follow the outline, which is fine.

## What They Learn

Language and communication development skills: Talking about pictures and concepts while a child uses a lacing card expands her vocabulary and promotes language development. For example, discuss the pictures with the child by naming them or asking her questions about various parts of the pictures: "What part will you lace next? This thing on the roof? What is it called? Yes, that's the chimney." You also can discuss the concepts and words involved in the lacing process, such as *front, back, over, under, inside, outside, outline,* and *edge*: "Now what will you do with the lace? Bring it under this hole and out this one? Yes, that will work."

## Extending the Learning

Children learn speech sounds gradually in their early years. In the beginning, some children may be hard to understand because they have not yet acquired all of the sounds of language. Children in the process of acquiring language skills can be expected to struggle with sounds. However, correcting a child's speech or having her start a word over again is not useful and may even inhibit language learning.

## What You Need

- ☐ material for the lacing board (such as a 9-inch square section of pegboard or a plastic lid)
- ☐ pattern from coloring book pictures or large-patterned wrapping paper
- ☐ pencil
- ☐ permanent markers or paint
- ☐ scissors
- ☐ glue
- ☐ hole punch
- ☐ cloth tape
- ☐ lacing materials (shoelaces, rug yarn, or leather)

## How to Make It

1. Draw pictures of common objects or cut out pictures from coloring books or wrapping paper.

2. For pegboard lacing boards, trace the pattern onto the pegboard with a pencil. Fill in the picture with permanent marker or paint.

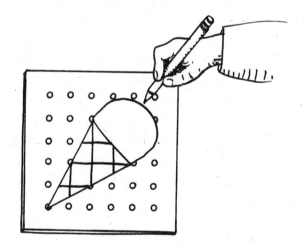

For plastic lid lacing cards, glue a picture to the lid. Punch holes around the outer edge of the picture or around the edge of the lid. If possible, cut the rim off the plastic lid so a hole punch can reach the outline. Tape around the edge.

3. Cut the lacing material into lengths of 15 to 18 inches. If you are using yarn, wrap the ends with tape to stiffen them and prevent fraying.

## Variation

Assemble a variety of household items children can use for lacing, such as colanders or slotted spoons. Toddlers will especially enjoy lacing these items.

Use long grasses, reeds, or grapevines soaked in water to lace a chain link fence with biodegradable materials.

GREEN IDEA • GREEN IDEA •

# Bucket Brigade

## Who

Toddlers

## About the Toy

This portable dump-and-fill toy encourages hand-eye coordination, small-muscle development, and problem-solving skills. Toddlers also enjoy carrying the bucket around and adding other toys to the collection.

## What They Learn

Physical and motor development and cognitive development skills: Toddlers naturally begin to seek out experiences that enhance their small-muscle development, such as putting things in and removing things from containers, and fitting things through different sizes of holes or openings. Toddlers also use their developing problem-solving skills to determine which objects fit through which holes in the bucket's lid. By repeating these types of tasks over and over, they are solidifying their knowledge base and are setting the stage for future learning.

## Extending the Learning

Although some toddlers will need your help fitting objects through the lid or removing the lid from the bucket, resist the temptation to immediately step in to help. With your guidance, most toddlers will become successful at these tasks. In addition, discussing the disappearance and reappearance of objects with a child encourages language development, reasoning, and the ability to make associations.

## What You Need

- ☐ large, clean plastic bucket with lid
- ☐ assorted objects (such as soft curlers, film canisters, small face cream containers, kitty treat containers, plastic cookie cutters, and small blocks)
- ☐ X-Acto knife or scissors
- ☐ markers
- ☐ tape

## How to Make It

1. Remove the lid from the bucket. On the lid, trace around each object you have collected.

2. Using an X-Acto knife or scissors, cut holes following the tracings on the lid. Test to make sure each object fits through its hole.

3. Use tape to cover any sharp edges around the holes.

4. Place objects inside the bucket and replace the lid.

Ask families to bring in ice cream buckets or oatmeal boxes to use in place of a plastic bucket.

GREEN IDEA • GREEN IDEA •

# Older Toddlers and Preschoolers

# Simple Lotto

## Who

Older toddlers and preschoolers

## About the Toy

Lotto teaches recognition of likenesses and differences. Matching pictures or patterns helps children learn visual discrimination, which is a prereading skill. This game can be played alone or in a group. When played in a group, the game provides opportunities for taking turns and cooperating with others.

Put three or four pictures on each lotto board to create a simple game for younger children (ages two to three). For older children, make lotto boards with six pictures on them.

To play lotto, place individual cards face down in a pile. Give each child a lotto board. Children take turns picking cards and searching all of the lotto boards for a match. Let the child who picks the card be the main searcher, but encourage all children to help find it. Children can continue playing until all of the boards are covered. If needed, remind children that the goal is to enjoy filling the boards as a group, not to be the first to cover a board.

## What They Learn

Cognitive development skills: As an older toddler or preschooler works with the lotto board, he is developing the ability to match pictures or patterns with similar characteristics, identify simple shapes, and identify and learn basic colors.

## Extending the Learning

One of the best ways to assess a child's level of cognitive development is through casual activities and games. You can use the lotto board to help determine a child's level of competence with specific skills as well as reinforce his learning. For example, as he works to match the pictures on the board, ask him yes-or-no questions about them: "Is this flower yellow? What about this flower?" Can he tell you whether or not the pictures are the same? Older preschoolers may even be able to group the pictures into specific categories, such as food items, clothing items, or toys.

## What You Need

☐ pictures

☐ eight unlined index cards (5 by 8 inches) or tagboard

☐ scissors

☐ glue

☐ ruler

☐ black marker

☐ clear contact paper

## How to Make It

1. Cut out matching sets of different pictures from gift-wrapping paper or wallpaper. One set is for the lotto boards, and the other set is for the matching cards. For younger children, you will need twenty-four pictures to make four lotto boards (three pictures on each board). For older children, you will need forty-eight pictures to make four lotto boards (six pictures on each board).

2. Draw lines on each index card to form six boxes (draw three or four boxes for younger children).

3. Create two index cards with identical pictures on them by gluing one of each matching picture to separate index cards. Cover with clear contact paper.

4. Leave one card uncut to use as the lotto board. Cut the second card along the lines to create the playing cards.

Instead of decorative paper, use photos from magazines showing the Earth's ecosystems.

GREEN IDEA • GREEN IDEA •

# Magnet Match-Ups

## Who

Older toddlers and preschoolers

## About the Toy

These lids provide an introduction to the workings of magnets. Toddlers will enjoy putting them on and taking them off a metal surface, such as a refrigerator door or a cookie sheet. Encourage older toddlers and preschoolers to match the patterns that look alike and put them next to each other on a refrigerator door or other metal surface. Older toddlers can use the lids to play concentration games on a metal surface or invent their own sorting games.

## What They Learn

Language and communication development skills: At this stage in their development, older toddlers and preschoolers typically have a speaking vocabulary of about 200 words. Toys such as these match-up lids, which have a variety of patterns and textures, encourage further language development. As children work with the lids, they pay close attention to the details involved in matching them and,

in the process, discover new words that describe what the lids look like and how they feel.

## Extending the Learning

As a preschooler examines and works to match the metal lids, talk with her about the patterns and what they look like. Use words such as *spotted, polka dot, square-patterned, diamond-patterned, flower-patterned, floral, plaid,* and *striped.* Say, for example, "There are some lids here with red polka dots on them. Which lids have red polka dots? Yes, those two have polka dots. They are a polka-dot pair." Also discuss any textures the fabrics may have, such as fuzzy, furry, silky, soft, smooth, scratchy, rough, bumpy, and hard.

## What You Need

- ☐ juice can lids
- ☐ scissors
- ☐ index cards (optional)
- ☐ magnetic tape
- ☐ tube container
- ☐ pattern and texture samples
- ☐ glue stick
- ☐ colorful contact paper (optional)

## How to Make It

1. Cut circles from the pattern and texture samples (two of each pattern or texture) to fit inside juice can lids. Consider using fabric scraps, wallpaper samples, or wrapping-paper patterns.

2. Glue a circle onto each lid. (If a sample is very delicate, first mount it on an index card, then cut it into a circle to fit the lid.)

3. Place a large piece of magnetic tape on the reverse side of each lid. Store the lids in a tube-like container.

Ask a local fabric store for scraps of fabric they would otherwise throw away.

GREEN IDEA • GREEN IDEA •

# Flexible Feely Board

## Who

Older toddlers and young preschoolers

## About the Toy

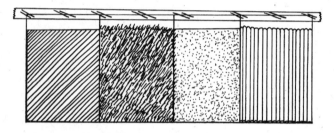

This feely board helps toddlers learn the characteristics of materials through their sense of sight and touch. Find a variety of contrasting textures to attach to the feely board. Display the board at the children's eye level so toddlers can touch it and visually explore it. Young preschoolers can be encouraged to test their language skills by playing a game that asks them to put on a blindfold, feel a texture on the board, and then guess what it is or describe what it feels like. For both age groups, make a variety of boards that can be changed as needed.

## What They Learn

Approaches to learning development skills: Toddlers and preschoolers are naturally curious and reflective, traits that help them learn about their world and how it works. Tactile experiences, that is, experiences during which children touch and manipulate various objects, offer the best kinds of learning experiences for children of this age.

## Extending the Learning

As a child touches the various textures on the feely board, he is learning the characteristics of materials. When you help describe the sensations he feels with his fingertips, he begins to associate textures with descriptive words, some of which may be new to him. For example, in describing a piece of sheepskin with wool on it, say, "This wool is soft. Do you feel how soft it is?" In describing sandpaper, you might say, "Rough. This sandpaper is very rough and scratchy." In the days ahead, listen for whether he applies these new descriptive terms to other objects he encounters in his environment.

## What You Need

☐ tagboard

☐ texture samples

☐ scissors

☐ ruler

☐ glue

☐ Velcro or tape

☐ shoebox for storage

## How to Make It

1. To make a feely board to which you can affix various textures, cut the tagboard into pieces that are approximately 5 by 7 inches. (You also can use the back of writing tablets or panty hose inserts to make the base of a feely board.)

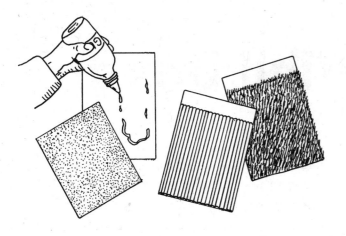

3. Invite older toddlers and three-year-olds to close their eyes when they want to play the feel-and-guess game. Store the feely boards in the shoebox.

## Variations

For a more permanent feely board, glue different textures onto a large piece of tagboard, leaving a 1-inch uncovered edge along all sides of the tagboard. Tape the board to the selected surface.

Use the Child-Safe Display Rack (see p. 200) for mounting the feely boards.

For older children, convert the feely boards to a matching game. Attach a strip of Velcro next to each texture. Cut small samples of the same textures that are used on the feely boards and place a strip of Velcro on the back of each one. Keep the small samples nearby in a container. Children can place the small samples next to matching textures on the board.

2. Cut each texture sample 1 inch shorter than the board. Consider using pieces of satin, sandpaper, scrubbing pads, fur, netting, foam, or wool. Glue a different texture sample onto each board, leaving a 1-inch space at the top of the board uncovered. This space can be used to mount the feely board to a surface (such as the refrigerator, a door, the side of a bookshelf, or a wall).

Ask a local hardware or lumber store for scraps of wood they would otherwise throw away.

# Feel-and-Tell Box

## Who

Older toddlers and preschoolers

## About the Toy

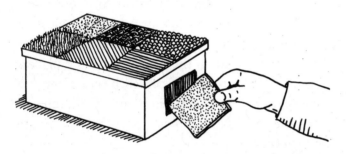

This box toy filled with interesting textures encourages children to identify items by touch and by sight. It helps develop awareness of different textures and the many words that can be used to describe them, such as *rough, smooth, bumpy,* and *furry.* Children also gain practice in using words and concepts that help them understand the idea of matching and finding pairs. Toddlers will enjoy playing with the texture samples; preschoolers can play the matching game described in the variation (on the following page).

## What They Learn

Cognitive development skills: Memory is a central process in children's cognitive development, beginning with simple short-term memory tasks such as the task associated with the Feel-and-Tell Box. First, a child reaches inside the box and feels one of the texture pieces. Before removing it from the box, she uses her memory of its texture to find its match by touching the pieces mounted on the lid. After the child has chosen a texture on the lid, she removes the piece from the box to see whether the two pieces are the same.

## Extending the Learning

Young children's memory skills increase with age. Most older toddlers and preschoolers will be able to recall and match simple objects by their characteristics using their senses of touch and sight. As you observe a child playing with the texture samples, you can reinforce her learning by helping her to think about and describe the different textures. Ask her, "Why are those two the same?" "How do they both feel?" "What else can you think of that feels furry like this?"

## What You Need

- ☐ shoebox with lid
- ☐ texture samples
- ☐ scissors
- ☐ cardboard or tagboard
- ☐ glue

## How to Make It

1. Cut two squares of each texture sample. Consider using steel wool, sandpaper, fabric scraps, and paper.

2. Glue a sample of each texture onto the lid of the shoebox.

4. In one end of the shoebox, cut a hole large enough for a child's hand. Put on the lid.

## Variation

Make a game that matches objects to pictures of the objects. Mount pictures of objects on a different shoebox lid. (You can use the shoebox from the activity described on the previous page.) Put the matching objects inside the shoebox. Objects to use include a small ball and a small car, a key, a comb, a block, a crayon, and a spoon.

3. Glue the remaining texture samples onto squares of cardboard or tagboard. Place them inside the shoebox.

Invite families to bring in scraps of fabric, ribbon, yarn, and other materials instead of throwing them away. Then you and the children can use them for art and other learning activities.

GREEN IDEA • GREEN IDEA

# Where's the Scoop?

## Who

Older toddlers and preschoolers

## About the Toy

This toy helps teach color matching and recognition as children match cutouts of scoops of ice cream to the cone of the same color. Finding the correct scoop shapes and putting them in outlines above the cone shapes encourages hand-eye coordination. The variation on the opposite page encourages number awareness and helps build number-recognition skills.

## What They Learn

Cognitive development skills: Beginning at around two years of age, children start to demonstrate an ability to use symbols, such as words and numbers, to represent real objects in their environment. As children match the colored ice-cream cutouts to the cones on the folder, they are learning to differentiate colors and color names.

## Extending the Learning

Your involvement in activities such as color matching can foster a child's learning. As you watch him work to match the colored scoops to the scoops on the folder, ask him questions, such as "Which scoops are pink?" and "What color is this scoop?" To extend the activity and his learning, ask him to show you other things that are the same colors, including clothing items you both are wearing. "What are you wearing that is blue?"

## What You Need

☐ construction paper in eight colors

☐ cone and scoop patterns (see opposite page)

☐ pencil

☐ scissors

☐ file folder

☐ glue

☐ black marker

☐ clear contact paper

☐ paper clip

☐ small plastic bag

## How to Make It

1. Trace the pattern of the cone and scoop onto construction paper, making one set from each color. Cut out the patterns.

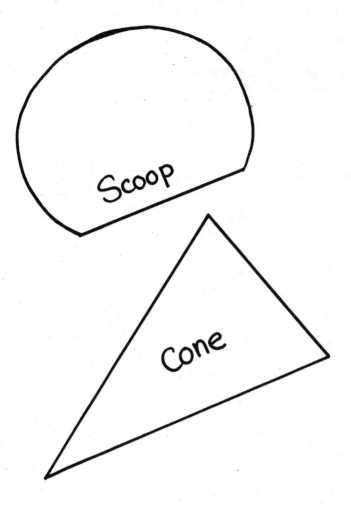

Scoop

Cone

4. Cover both sides of the scoop shapes with clear contact paper. Place them in a small plastic bag for storage. Clip the bag to the edge of the file folder.

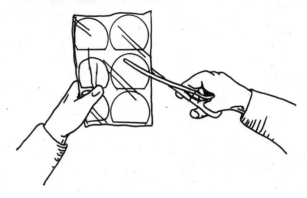

## Variation

Use this activity as a number matching game. Use wipe-off crayons or washable markers to number each cone from 1 to 8. Place a corresponding number of stickers or small dots on one side of each scoop.

For an easy number match, keep the color of the stickers or small dots consistent with the color of the cone and scoop. For a more difficult game, vary the marker color.

If you add the dots or stickers *after* the clear contact paper has been placed over the cones and scoops, you can alter them and change the sets or combinations.

2. Glue the cone shapes onto the file folder. Draw a cross-hatch design on them. Draw the outline of a scoop above each cone.

3. Cover the file folder with clear contact paper.

Using ice cream cones instead of bowls to serve ice cream is a great way to help the environment, and they taste great too! Plastic bowls end up in the garbage, and washable bowls require a run through the dishwasher. Cones are eaten, producing no waste and requiring no dish washing—though children may need to wash their faces.

GREEN IDEA • GREEN IDEA

# Shoebox Train

## Who

Older toddlers and preschoolers

## About the Toy

This Shoebox Train provides older toddlers and preschoolers with a chance to help create toys they can use in various types of play. Older toddlers may enjoy putting their toys and stuffed animals into the boxes and using the train for fill-and-dump games. Preschoolers may use them to enhance make-believe or fantasy play.

## What They Learn

Physical and motor development and approaches to learning development skills: Older toddlers are furthering their physical skills when they use the shoebox trains as pull toys and for fill-and-dump games. Through fantasy play involving the train, preschoolers are demonstrating their abilities to use props to create new scripts of their lives. Fantasy play gives preschool-age children opportunities to test their existing knowledge as well as to explore new ways of thinking about things and the world around them.

## Extending the Learning

As older toddlers play with the train, you will notice how they seem to enjoy repeating physical movements over and over with little encouragement from you. Through repetition, children are learning to coordinate and refine their movements. While observing preschool-age children play with the train, listen for their emerging language skills. You can encourage further development of these skills by occasionally asking open-ended questions about the train, such as "Who is the driver of your train?" or "Where are the animals on the train going?"

## What You Need

☐ shoeboxes of various sizes
☐ markers
☐ paper circles
☐ glue
☐ scissors
☐ yarn or string
☐ drinking straws
☐ large button
☐ magazines

## How to Make It

1. Let the children use the markers to decorate the boxes. Children can also cut out pictures

from magazines to glue to the boxes. Glue on the paper wheels. (If you want the wheels to turn, use cardboard circles and attach them with brass fasteners.)

2. Poke holes at both ends of each shoebox. Make only one hole in the box that will be the caboose.

3. Connect the boxes with pieces of yarn or string. Run the yarn or string between the cars through drinking straws to create links that will not become slack. Knot yarn securely inside each box.

4. Attach an 18-inch-long piece of yarn to the front car and tie a large button onto the end of it to serve as a handle.

Ask families and friends to donate shoeboxes. If space allows, collect reusable materials year round and keep them in a designated closet.

GREEN IDEA · GREEN IDEA ·

# Water-Play Kit

## Who

Older toddlers and preschoolers

## About the Toy

Water play encourages children to experiment with scientific principles such as why certain objects sink or float. Older toddlers and preschoolers can use the cups for pouring and investigate using basters, funnels, and tubing. Model how to use the basters or eyedroppers to draw up water and how to cover the tops of tubes with a finger to pick up water and then drop it.

## What They Learn

Sensory perception and cognitive development skills: Water play is a satisfying and soothing activity for young children. Often enjoyed as a sensory experience, water play also engages children in cognitive experiences that involve experimenting with cause and effect, measurement, and quantity. Experiences such as these contribute to children's understanding of more sophisticated concepts later on, for example, that ½ cup of water is the same amount of water in any shape container.

## Extending the Learning

Water play offers many learning opportunities for young children. Watch a child as she discovers that some objects float and some do not. When she creates a whirlpool with her hand, some of the water rises and spills over the side of the dishpan—creating both a physical exercise and an exercise in beginning physics. When weather permits, move water-play activities outdoors. Children's engagement in water play takes on different qualities outdoors, since there is less concern about splashing and spilling, allowing for more creative and boisterous experimentation.

## What You Need

☐ water-play items

☐ plastic dishpan

☐ water

☐ jelly roll pan

☐ container to hold water items

## How to Make It

1. Put water-play items on the jelly roll pan. Consider using measuring cups, spoons, large plastic lids, funnels, basters, eyedroppers, sieves, strainers, small pieces of plastic tubing, and small plastic jars. Make sure the items are clean.

2. Fill the dishpan one-fourth to one-third full of tepid water. Place the dishpan and the water-play toys on the jelly roll pan. Place the pan and toys on a towel or rug, if desired.

*Note:* With proper supervision, you can easily use the Water-Play Kit indoors as well as out. The younger the child is, the smaller the amount of water you should use to begin with.

## Variations

Assemble additional Water-Play Kits for a variety of activities. Consider the following:

**Washing clothes or dishes:** small packet of soap (Ivory Flakes, Ivory Snow, or Dreft), eggbeater to mix suds, container and plastic pitcher for rinse water, clothes or dishes to wash, bath towel to lay washed items on or clothespins to hang clothes.

**Color mixing:** small plastic jars, eyedroppers, plastic spoons, food coloring or a few drops of tempera paint (optional: items to dye, such as large pasta, eggs or eggshells, scraps of paper).

Invite children to bring in items they think will sink or float, such as sponges, corks, rocks, small boats, wood pieces, and metal spoons.

GREEN IDEA · GREEN IDEA

# Squish Bags

## Who

Older toddlers and preschoolers

## About the Toy

These Squish Bags provide opportunities for sensory exploration for toddlers and preschoolers. Children can squeeze and manipulate the bags to feel the textures of the materials inside them and blend the colors together to see how colors are mixed together. Consider adding more food coloring to darken or change the colors. The bags can also serve as a clean introduction to fingerpainting for children who may be reluctant to experiment with real fingerpaints.

**!** **Caution:** This activity requires close supervision.

## What They Learn

Sensory perception development skills: Older toddlers and preschoolers are still learning primarily through their senses of sight, sound, touch, taste, and smell. For example, they will squeeze, pull, flatten, and tug at the Squish Bags to learn more about the materials inside them. They also will observe how the colors in the bags move and change to become new colors the more they manipulate the bags.

## Extending the Learning

Activities involving the Squish Bags can also enhance language development and fine-motor skills. Ask a child to describe what he is doing to the bag and how his actions affect the colors inside. Is he making new colors? What are they? You also can suggest a few tasks to challenge his small-muscle skills, such as "Try pinching the bag in its corners with your fingers to see what happens to the colors" and "Show me again how you drew that long line with your finger all the way across the bag."

## What You Need

☐ cornstarch

☐ water

☐ saucepan

☐ whisk

☐ measuring cups

☐ access to a stove away from the children

☐ food coloring

☐ small- or medium-size, heavy-duty plastic bags

## How to Make It

1. Use the whisk to mix 2 cups of cold water with ½ cup of cornstarch in the saucepan. Cook over medium heat, stirring constantly until the mixture thickens. Allow the mixture to cool.

2. Divide half the mixture into bags.

3. Squirt in several drops of food coloring (use just one color in each bag).

4. Add more of the mixture so the food coloring is surrounded.

5. Gently squeeze as much air as possible from the bag and seal it shut. Let children manipulate the bag. If desired, open the bag and add a second color. Reseal as before.

The colored mixture in the bags can also be used as homemade fingerpaints.

# Twist and Turn

## Who

Toddlers and preschoolers

## About the Toy

Place a container holding the jars and lids on a table or the floor. Children can unscrew the tops from the jars and mix them up, and then find the ones that fit and screw them back together again. One child can play with the lids and jars by herself, or two children can work together, taking turns picking a lid and trying to find its matching jar.

## What They Learn

Physical and motor development skills: At this stage in their physical development, toddlers and preschoolers have mastered the pincer grasp, the use of the thumb and index finger to pick up small objects. In addition, most can also turn knobs and faucets and play with screw-on-type toys, such as the containers used in this activity. While a child

works to screw and unscrew the lids, she not only is refining her fine-motor skills, but also is practicing other skills, such as hand-eye coordination and visual discrimination.

## Extending the Learning

Although most children between eighteen and twenty-four months begin to show a preference for using their right or left hand while performing a few select activities (for example, reaching for things or turning the pages of a book) they can still perform most activities with both hands. In general, signs of hand dominance—the clear preference of one hand over the other—do not appear until a child is about five years old.

## What You Need

- ☐ container (such as a plastic bowl with a lid or a shoebox)
- ☐ eight to ten assorted small plastic jars with screw-on lids
- ☐ 3-by-5-inch index card
- ☐ marker
- ☐ tape
- ☐ clear contact paper

## How to Make It

1. Clean and dry the jars and lids. Be sure each lid fits only one jar.

2. Place the assortment of jars and lids in a container.

3. Create a label for the container by drawing a picture of jars and lids on the index card. Tape the label to the container in a prominent place and cover it with clear contact paper.

Ask families for empty jars from cosmetic products, spices, baking or food items, baby products, suntan lotion, and travel-size jars of shampoo and lotions.

GREEN IDEA · GREEN IDEA ·

# Keys for Learning

## Who

Older toddlers and preschoolers

## About the Toy

To use this toy, prop the board with all of the hooks in it against a wall or on a chair, then select a set of key outline cards and keys. Put the outline cards on the hooks. Encourage the children to examine the keys carefully, noticing the shape of the top and bottom of each key. As children put the keys on the hooks, trying to find keys that match the picture outline on each hook, they are refining hand-eye coordination and small-motor skills. Younger children may simply put the keys on the hooks and ignore matching the shapes, which is fine. Older children can be encouraged to match keys of different colors to colored outlines or to match the jagged side of the outline to the actual key shape.

## What They Learn

Cognitive development skills: One of the cognitive skills older toddlers and preschoolers are developing has to do with attention, or their ability to focus on tasks for longer periods of time before becoming bored. Whereas younger toddlers may still wander around a room, shifting their attention from one activity to another, older toddlers and preschoolers are more likely to give this activity with keys their full attention before moving on to something new.

## Extending the Learning

Young children enjoy playing with keys, and this activity is another fun way children can play with and explore keys. You can learn a lot about a child's fine-motor skills by watching how successful he is with placing the keys on the hooks. If he is struggling to match the keys with their outlines on the board, consider adjusting the activity by using keys that are obviously different in shape; if he needs more of a challenge, use keys that are similar and make the outline of each key very precise.

## What You Need

- ☐ 8-by-10-inch plywood board
- ☐ sharp tool or small drill to start holes
- ☐ ruler
- ☐ L-shaped screw-in hooks (about ¹/₁₆-inch size)
- ☐ pliers (optional)
- ☐ index cards (4 by 6 inches) or tagboard per set
- ☐ old keys of various sizes and shapes

- ☐ fine-tipped colored markers
- ☐ scissors
- ☐ clear contact paper
- ☐ hole punch

## How to Make It

1. Use a sharp tool or drill to start making the holes in the plywood. Use pegboard and hooks as an alternative. Make two rows of three small holes. Leave about 2½ inches between each of the holes and approximately 4 inches between rows. Twist the hooks into the holes. A pair of pliers will make the task easier. Be sure the hooks do not go through the back of the plywood.

2. Cut index cards or tagboard into 2-by-3-inch pieces. Trace around a different key on each card. Make a dot in the keyhole. Cover cards with clear contact paper.

3. Punch holes on the dot of each key outline card. If you are making multiple sets, you may want to color code the cards and keys that go together.

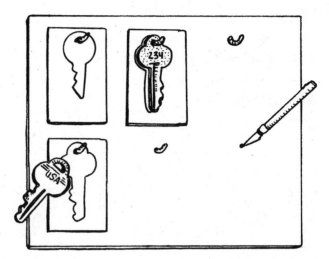

Old metal keys may contain lead. Do not allow children to place metal keys in their mouths. Consider making paper cutouts of keys for young children to match to the cards.

# Things to String

## Who

Older toddlers and preschoolers

## About the Toy

Set out containers of plastic tubes and large rubber washers—make several sets so children can work together. Allow the children to work with the materials in any way they choose, or you can model stringing beads on a section of tubing. Stringing activities enhance children's hand-eye coordination and small-muscle control. In addition, you can enhance their sensory development by adding the tubing and washers to water-play activities.

## What They Learn

Physical and motor development skills: The ability to string beads is a fairly advanced fine-motor skill that most children do not master until around age four. This prestringing activity can make a child's first attempts at stringing beads more successful by avoiding the frustration caused by standard laces.

## Extending the Learning

Determine, in advance, the level of a child's fine-motor skills and fashion the toy accordingly to allow for maximum success. Toddlers will be most successful stringing items such as large rubber washers, keys with large holes, or keys on key rings onto lengths of plastic tubing. Preschoolers can string metal washers and large beads onto thinner tubing, shoelaces, or wrapping cord.

## What You Need

**FOR TODDLERS:**

☐ lengths of plastic tubing

☐ large rubber washers with holes

☐ scissors

☐ tape

☐ spools

☐ keys with large holes or keys on key rings

**FOR PRESCHOOLERS:**

☐ thin tubing, shoelaces, or wrapping cord

☐ metal washers

☐ tape

☐ assorted beads

☐ various containers

## How to Make It

1. Cut tubing or string into sections that are 18 to 24 inches long.

2. Form a stopper by tying one end of each tube or string around a washer. Tubing and washers come in different thicknesses and are available in hardware or plumbing supply stores. If you are using string, put tape around the free end to make threading easier and to prevent fraying.

3. Set out various sizes of washers, buttons, and beads. Preschoolers can help sort the items into containers for storage.

**Caution:** To avoid spreading illnesses, provide each child with a tube and sanitize the tubes after each use. Be certain that the beads and washers are too large to swallow. This activity requires close supervision.

Use rubber washers and tubes again in the water table. Children can blow bubbles through tubing and string the washers onto the tubes.

GREEN IDEA · GREEN IDEA

# Clothespin Capers

## Who

Older toddlers and preschoolers

## About the Toy

These clothespin toys provide toddlers with opportunities to fill and dump as well as to refine hand-eye coordination skills. If you choose to draw faces on the clothespins, older toddlers and preschoolers can use the clothespins in dramatic play. If you place matching colored tape, numbers, or symbols on both the clothespins and the containers, preschoolers can play matching games by matching the colors, numbers, letters, names, or tiny pictures on the clothespins to the containers.

## What They Learn

Physical and motor development and approaches to learning development skills: Older toddlers will use the clothespins to work on fine-motor tasks such as fitting slip-on or clip-on clothespins onto the rims of various containers. Preschoolers, who are more advanced in their play, will have no trouble inventing scenarios for families of clothespin people to act out.

## Extending the Learning

Many experts consider the preschool years to be the "golden age" of symbolic, or dramatic, play. When children this age use props and toys to work out their ideas of how the world works with other children, the play takes on an added dimension and falls within the category of sociodramatic play. You can learn a great deal about a child by listening to her as she engages in sociodramatic play, since it's how she tests her existing models of the world and how she forms new models.

## What You Need

☐ slip-on or clip-on clothespins (depending on the ages of the children)

☐ containers with lids

☐ scissors

☐ markers

☐ a variety of colored tape

☐ stickers

## How to Make It

### FOR TODDLERS:

1. Cut one or more holes in each of the lids.

2. Make some holes big enough to allow the

clothespins to slip through and some that are smaller so that they hold the clothespins. Draw faces on the clothespins, if desired.

## FOR PRESCHOOLERS:

1. Depending on the skill level of the children, follow either the directions above or the directions below for creating matching games.

2. Make matching games by placing matching colored tape, numbers, or symbols on both the clip-on clothespins and the container.

Consider using clean lids and containers from cottage cheese cartons, milk cartons cut in half, or small boxes.

# Styrofoam Pounding Bench

## Who

Older toddlers and preschoolers

## About the Toy

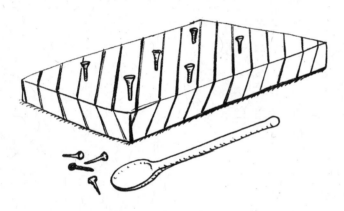

This bench pounding toy is made from a common packaging item, demonstrating to children a creative way of reusing materials. Set out large, heavy-duty sections of Styrofoam used for packing appliances, televisions, and other electronics. Also set out containers of colored golf tees and tools that can be used as mallets, such as wooden spoons or small hammers from pounding toys. Encourage the children to practice pounding the golf tees into sections of Styrofoam. Children can then pound in the tees as far as they like and help remove and return them to the storage containers when they are finished. Suggest to older preschoolers that they count how many tees they pounded as they remove them from the Styrofoam.

## What They Learn

Physical and motor development skills: By the time most children are preschool age, gender differences in motor development begin to become more pronounced. Whereas boys tend to excel in gross-motor activities, girls tend to excel in fine-motor activities. Fine-motor activities such as pounding small objects into wood, pegboards, or Styrofoam are ones both girls and boys enjoy, and they give preschoolers good practice with hand-eye coordination.

## Extending the Learning

Although children this age may begin showing an aptitude for either gross-motor or fine-motor activities, offer all children equal opportunities to practice both kinds of physical skills on a regular basis. For example, if a child works with the pounding bench in the morning, make sure he is involved in gross-motor learning experiences later in the day. Be sure to recognize a child's successes as well. You might say, for example, "You pounded that tee all the way into the Styrofoam!"

## What You Need

☐ large, heavy-duty Styrofoam blocks

☐ X-Acto knife or small saw

☐ golf tees and container

- ☐ contact paper
- ☐ bowl or resealable plastic bag
- ☐ two small mallets or wooden spoons

## How to Make It

1. Cut the Styrofoam into sections about 1½ by 2 feet. Cover sections with contact paper to reduce shredding and make cleanup easier.

2. Collect golf tees and put them into the container. Set them out with the Styrofoam bench and the mallets (small hammers or wooden spoons, for example).

**!** **Caution:** Be sure to keep the small pieces away from infants and young toddlers, who might put them in their mouths.

When the Styrofoam can no longer be used as a pounding bench, help further older children's experience with recycling by having them break the Styrofoam into small pieces. They can then use the pieces to create sculptures by connecting the pieces with straws, toothpicks, or other interesting and colorful materials.

GREEN IDEA · GREEN IDEA ·

# Take-Apart Teddy

## Who

Older toddlers and preschoolers

## About the Toy

These bear figures promote fine-motor and thinking skills as children take them apart and put them back together. The toys provide tactile and sensory experiences and call attention to the body parts of the bear, how they fit together, and their names. Children may also enjoy using the torsos, limbs, and features to play mix-and-match games. Keep the body parts, bows, and clothing together in a large plastic container or basket for easy access.

## What They Learn

Language and communication development skills: Children's development of language and vocabulary is central to their learning after about two years of age. Activities that foster and support language development take advantage of a child's interest in describing the world around her and in her growing ability to figure out her place within it.

## Extending the Learning

Almost any activity a child is involved in can support her language development, depending on how much you engage her. For example, as a child works to take apart the bear and put it back together, ask her open-ended questions about what she is doing: "Which part of the bear did you just take off of him?" or "What would happen if you put the bear's arm down at the bottom, where his leg used to be? How would he walk if you did that?" As important, leave opportunities for her to ask questions of you as well.

## What You Need

- ☐ large piece of brown felt
- ☐ small pieces of red, green, blue, yellow, and/or orange felt
- ☐ pencil
- ☐ scissors
- ☐ fabric marker
- ☐ Velcro
- ☐ fake fur or fabric scraps
- ☐ needle and thread (optional)

## How to Make It

1. Make a copy of the bear pattern (p. 66) and trace the pieces onto brown felt.

2. Cut out the felt pieces. With the fabric marker, draw a face on the head.

3. Cut small pieces of Velcro and sew them to the front and the back of the body parts, as shown on the pattern.

4. Trace the bow tie pattern on a small piece of colored felt or decorative fabric and cut it out. Attach Velcro to the back of it. Make several bow ties in different colors.

5. Cut several circles from the fake fur or fabric scraps to use as clothes. Make the circles approximately the same size as the part of the bear figure it will cover. Attach Velcro pieces to the back of the clothes.

## Variations

Make patterns for other animals. Use drawings from coloring books or picture books for inspiration. For three- and four-year-olds, use buttons or snaps in addition to Velcro to help teach the small-motor skills needed to work these fasteners.

Borrowing books from the library is free and helps save trees. Visit the library to learn more about bears and about plants and animals native to your area. Do bears live nearby?

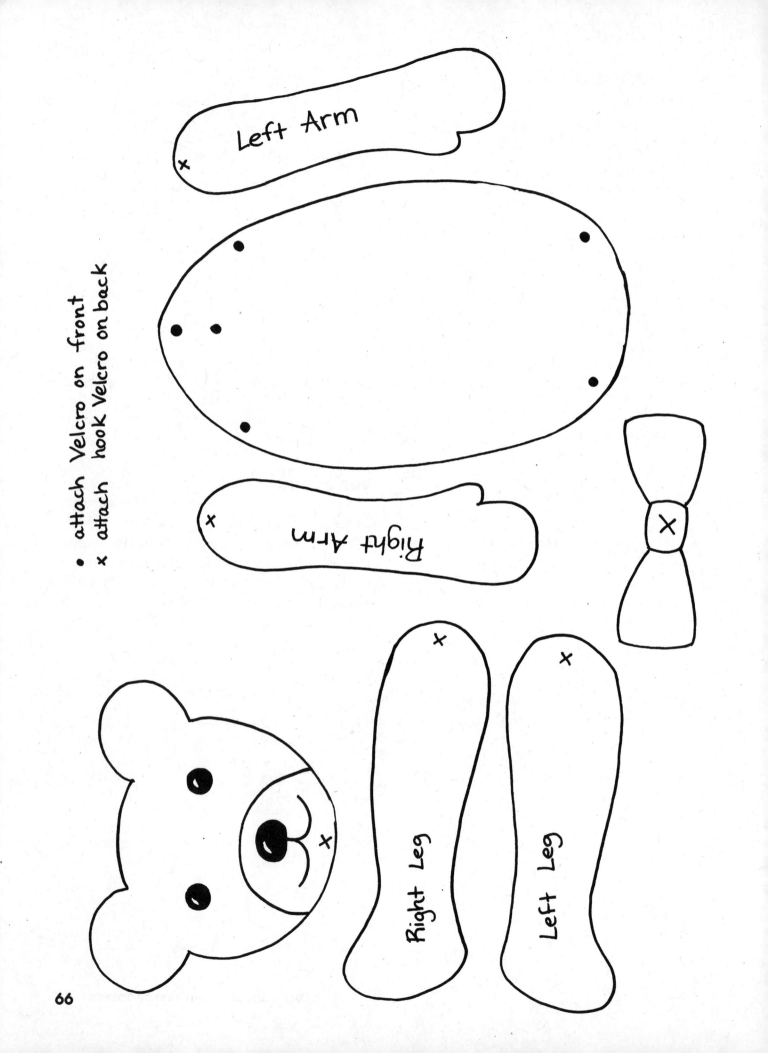

Left Arm

Right Arm

Right Leg

Left Leg

• attach Velcro on front
× attach hook Velcro on back

66

# Toddlers, Preschoolers, and Schoolagers

# Picture Puzzle

## Who

Toddlers, preschoolers, and schoolagers

## About the Toy

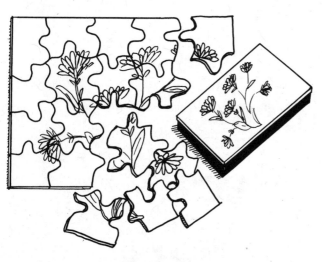

Puzzles provide many learning opportunities for children. Puzzles help foster problem-solving skills and learning about how parts fit together to make a whole. Children's visual discrimination skills are enhanced as they learn to distinguish shapes and colors. Puzzles also help develop children's hand-eye coordination and their sorting and matching skills. Allowing children to help in the process of creating puzzles encourages their creativity and enhances their self-esteem.

## What They Learn

Social and emotional development skills: Although children between the ages of two and four years old are working to develop their sense of autonomy and independence, most exhibit the self-control needed to play with and get along with others. Group experiences, such as assembling puzzles with others, give children opportunities to practice and try out their emerging social skills.

## Extending the Learning

When observing children engaged in cooperative learning experiences, listen to the words they use and the behaviors they exhibit. If a child is having difficulty with impulse control, use positive language to gently guide him to more acceptable behaviors. For example, rather than saying, "Don't grab the piece from him," say, "If you'd like that puzzle piece, try asking him nicely for it; he may just give it to you next time."

## What You Need

☐ magazines with colorful photographs and pictures

☐ tagboard or cardboard

☐ scissors

☐ glue

☐ clear contact paper

☐ flat box and cover or a large envelope

## How to Make It

1. Cut out a magazine picture. Glue it onto the tagboard or cardboard and cover it with clear contact paper.

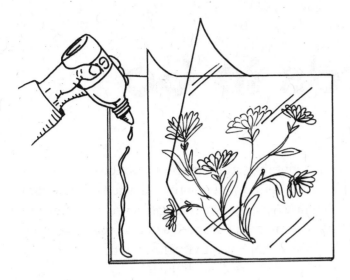

2. Cut the magazine picture into puzzle pieces. Cut large, simple pieces for toddlers. As children's ages and abilities increase, cut more, smaller puzzle pieces.

3. Draw or glue a likeness of the puzzle on the box lid or envelope. Store the puzzle inside the box or envelope.

## Variations

To help toddlers and other children who can benefit from it, create various borders for the puzzles. Children can then use the borders to help them put the puzzles together. There are three possible ways of making borders for the puzzles:

1. To create a border around the outside of the puzzle, use two pieces of cardboard, both pieces being 1 to 2 inches larger than the picture. Center and glue the picture onto one of the cardboard pieces. Cut out the picture. Glue the frame that remains to the other piece of uncut cardboard. Cut the picture into puzzle pieces. Children can then put the puzzle together inside the border without the frustration of the pieces slipping around.

2. With a felt-tip marker, trace the puzzle shapes onto the bottom of a flat box. The tracing marks will show how the pieces fit together.

3. Trace the outline of the puzzle onto the bottom of a flat box that is larger than the puzzle. Glue a heavy piece of yarn or cord onto the outline of the puzzle. Allow the glue to dry completely. Children can then put the puzzle together inside the yarn boundary without the frustration of the pieces slipping around.

Puzzles can be made from an unlimited number of materials. Consider using labels from food cans or boxes, kids' drawings, traced pictures, road maps (for schoolagers), and enlarged photographs of individuals or groups of children.

GREEN IDEA · GREEN IDEA ·

# Felt Boards to Go

## Who

Toddlers, preschoolers, and schoolagers

## About the Toy

Felt boards offer children a variety of cognitive, manipulative, sensory, and creative experiences, and they can be used in both traditional and unique ways. You can use cutout characters and a felt board to retell favorite stories or as a counting activity that involves matching objects to numerals. You can spell names and words with felt letters or use the figures to discuss body parts, feelings, or actions. Individually, a child can use a felt board to make pictures or designs with the cutouts or to match patterns on cue cards. The box-top felt boards and the felt boards in the variations section are easy to transport for an additional activity on field trips or for use outdoors.

## What They Learn

Cognitive development skills: Children of this age are developing more and more complex thinking skills, but they still learn best through tactile experiences. As they manipulate the felt pieces, children are developing a stronger sense of shapes and the meaning of numbers while at the same time expressing their creativity through the designs and pictures they create with the felt pieces.

## Extending the Learning

To get a better idea of a child's understanding of shapes and numbers, ask her to perform a few tasks with the felt pieces. Say, for example, "Put three red circles on your board," or "See if you can find the shapes to make a snowman." If she is able to perform the tasks with little difficulty, make a design on the board and ask her to copy it. As she does so, ask her how many shapes she will need and the color of each. If the tasks seem too challenging, work together to make a simple design on the board. Explain your actions as you go along: "I'm thinking of putting a green square on the board. Which piece should I pick up from the pile?"

## What You Need

- ☐ box with lid, such as a gift or shirt box (about 10 by 14 inches)
- ☐ felt or Velcro to fit the lid
- ☐ material for cutouts (such as felt, Velcro, or flannel)
- ☐ glue
- ☐ scissors
- ☐ markers
- ☐ resealable plastic bags
- ☐ labels

## How to Make It

1. Glue the felt or Velcro to the inside of the box lid.

2. Use the chosen material to make cutouts of shapes, designs, letters, and numerals. You can also buy precut felt letters and numbers.

3. For retelling favorite stories, trace storybook characters and props onto the chosen material. If you have old storybooks, cut out images of the characters, glue a small piece of Velcro or felt onto the back, and use them for retelling stories.

4. Store the pieces for each story in a separate resealable plastic bag and label it with the story title and identifying picture. Also store cutouts of shapes, designs, and patterns in individualized bags.

## Variations

You can also make a felt board by wrapping felt, flannel, or Velcro around heavy tagboard or sheets of cardboard that are approximately 9 by 12 inches. Store the board and cutouts in a large manila envelope.

Create an easel-style felt board using a cardboard mailing box. Cut away all cardboard from the box except the front and back and one long side of the box that creates a hinge. Cover the entire outside surface with felt, flannel, or Velcro and glue it in place. Glue a business-size envelope or a 7-by-10-inch manila envelope to each inside part of the cardboard, leaving the flap exposed. Use the envelopes to store the cutouts.

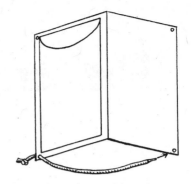

Poke a hole in each of the four corners of the board when it is laid out flat. Bend the board into a tent shape, felt side out. Thread two lengths of 12-inch-long string or shoelace through the front holes and then through the back holes. Tie each end into knots large enough to prevent them from slipping through the holes. This makes a neat two-person, easel-style felt board or an easy store-and-tote flannel board for individual children.

Another easy way to create an easel-style felt board is to cut two equal-size pieces of sturdy cardboard. Create a hinge by taping together the two long sides of the cardboard pieces. Use duct tape to make the hinge strong. To allow for the bend in the hinge, leave approximately ½ inch of space between the two cardboard pieces. Cover the entire outside surface with felt, flannel, or Velcro and glue it in place. Proceed as in the previous variation.

> Make a felt board using bolt ends (the cardboard rectangles around which fabric is wrapped in fabric stores). For easy storage, staple one end of the felt, flannel, or Velcro to the bolt and roll the felt around the bolt.

GREEN IDEA · GREEN IDEA ·

# Instant Paintbrush

## Who

Toddlers, preschoolers, and schoolagers

## About the Toy

These unique paintbrushes, which are easy to make and to use, are low-cost alternatives to purchased paintbrushes. By attaching clothespins to cut-up sponges, the clothespins become the handles of brushes children can use at a table or easel, or out-doors. These paintbrushes also make painting less messy, thereby encouraging even reluctant painters to give painting a try.

## What They Learn

Approaches to learning development skills: Children between the ages of two and four years old are naturally curious—about everything! Letting children experiment with a variety of art materials, for example, satisfies their need for tactile experiences and creative exploration.

## Extending the Learning

As a child creates with the different paintbrushes, help him expand his vocabulary as well as his thinking skills by asking him questions about the brushes and the marks they leave on the paper. Ask him to describe how the feather feels, guiding him to use words such as *soft* and *tickly*. Ask him how the sponge and the cotton balls are different. How are the marks they leave on the paper different? These types of open-ended questions (questions without right or wrong answers) require him to reflect on his actions and articulate his thoughts. Which brush does he like the best? Why? What would happen if he clipped two kinds of materials in the same clothespin? How would the marks on the paper change?

## What You Need

☐ sponges or other materials (such as feathers, leaves, pom-poms, cotton balls, or pieces of string)

☐ scissors

☐ clip clothespins

☐ tempera paints

☐ muffin tin or assorted small plastic containers with covers

☐ paper

## How to Make It

1. Cut the sponges into a variety of sizes and shapes. Assemble the other materials you want to use. Clip the materials to the clothespins.

2. Pour tempera paint into the containers. Leave two or three containers empty to hold extra brushes.

Almost any item—from a feather to a leaf—can be turned into a fun paintbrush that inspires children's creativity.

GREEN IDEA • GREEN IDEA •

# Picture-and-Word Books

## Who

Toddlers, preschoolers, and schoolagers

## About the Toy

Because the pages of these books are made from resealable plastic bags, you can customize them to meet each child's level of development and interest. For toddlers, make books that include pictures of things that are familiar to them. Let the children turn the pages and tell you what they see or ask questions for you to answer. Change the pictures to reflect their learning and development. Have older toddlers and young preschoolers tell you stories about the pictures. Older preschoolers and school-agers can make their own books to share with each other or make books for younger children. All the children will enjoy books containing pictures of their family members, either to share with others or to take comfort in on difficult days.

## What They Learn

Language and communication development skills: Reading with another person helps children learn new words and concepts and gain information about the world around them. Reading also fosters social and communication skills. In addition, the more children are exposed to books and other print materials, the more quickly they are apt to grasp the concept that letters are symbols that form the words they speak. Their more advanced fine-motor skills also make this the perfect age to learn what books are all about—how they are held, how the pages are turned, and that the text is read from left to right.

## Extending the Learning

The very best way to interest a child in books and foster key prereading skills such as print awareness and listening skills, is to read to her every day. By making the time for reading and by reading with excitement and enthusiasm, you show her that you enjoy reading and that reading is very important to you. Regular trips to the library will become much-anticipated events, and will expose her to the many wonderful children's books available.

## What You Need

- ☐ four to eight resealable plastic bags
- ☐ tagboard
- ☐ scissors
- ☐ glue
- ☐ magazines with pictures, snapshots, or drawing materials
- ☐ needle and thread or sewing machine
- ☐ bias tape or cloth tape (optional)
- ☐ stapler
- ☐ clear plastic tape

## How to Make It

1. Cut a piece of tagboard about ⅛ inch smaller than the inside measurements of the plastic bags.

2. Glue images to each side of the tagboard pieces. Consider collecting images from magazines and snapshots, or draw them yourself. Leave space on the tagboard pieces for recording stories or labeling the pictures.

3. Slip each piece of tagboard into its own plastic bag, with the open end of the bag at the top. Stack the bags with all the openings at the top.

4. Sew the left sides of the plastic bags securely together. For optimal strength, cover the binding side with bias tape or cloth tape before sewing. Schoolagers can make books by stapling the sides together first and then taping over the staples.

5. Change the images and material in the plastic bags to create theme books that will engage the children. Consider the following ideas:

*People books:* Pictures of each child with his or her name written underneath encourage self-esteem and name recognition. Extend this idea by adding pictures of the child's family, home, pets, and friends.

*Feelings books:* Pictures of children showing different emotions help children identify or discuss a particular emotion. Ask questions to prompt discussion, for example, "Are you feeling sad like this boy?" "Are you feeling angry like this child?" "What can we do to help you feel better?"

*Feely books:* Attach different textures to the tagboard pieces and insert them into the resealable plastic bags. Cut out a small circle in the middle of each plastic bag. Infants and toddlers can touch the textures and discuss them with you, using descriptive words such as *smooth, rough,* and *fuzzy.*

*Action books:* Use each plastic page to store items that can be removed, such as small puzzles, matching games, tricks, lacing cards, or origami instructions and paper.

Consider using items such as coloring books, counting books, or books on the seasons to create theme books. Use the theme books to convey concepts, for example, self-care or taking care of nature. You can also create theme books using natural items, such as leaves, feathers, or flowers.

GREEN IDEA • GREEN IDEA

# Stack-a-Lot Containers

## Who

Toddlers, preschoolers, and schoolagers

## About the Toy

These stacking containers help children understand size differences, shapes, and word concepts. They encourage exploration, creative building play, and small-muscle skills development. They also give children hands-on experiences with physical characteristics that enable them to form new concepts, for example, that round objects roll.

## What They Learn

Physical and motor and cognitive development skills: Children may play with these open-ended stacking toys in very different ways, depending on their ages, interests, and stages of fine-motor development. Toddlers may practice putting the containers inside one another, while preschoolers may enjoy simply rolling them across the floor. Schoolagers, on the other hand, may use the containers to measure size differences by ordering them from tallest to shortest or smallest to largest.

## Extending the Learning

As you watch how children of different ages play with these stacking toys, note which activities seem to be most appealing to which age groups. Then when a toddler loses interest in playing with the containers one way, you will be able to guide him into thinking about and playing with the containers in an entirely new way. For example, you might ask him, "Have you thought about what might happen if you rolled these containers across the floor? Which one do you think will go the farthest?"

## What You Need

- ☐ a variety of empty cans, plastic containers, boxes, or tubes in different sizes
- ☐ colorful contact paper
- ☐ scissors
- ☐ heavy tape

## How to Make It

1. Clean the containers thoroughly. If you are using metal cans, cover the rim with heavy tape to make sure there are no sharp edges.

2. Cut colorful contact paper 1 inch longer than each container. Cover each container with the contact paper, folding the extra over the rim.

> Instead of using contact paper to decorate the containers, use scraps of cloth and construction paper or pictures cut from old magazines. Glue pictures and construction paper scraps on the containers.
>
> GREEN IDEA · GREEN IDEA

# Boats and
# Other Floatables

## Who

Toddlers, preschoolers, and schoolagers

## About the Toy

Boats and other floatable toys give children hands-on experience with the concepts of floating and sinking. Older children may be interested in learning about water displacement, the concept that the volume of water displaced by a boat must weigh more than the boat to keep the boat from sinking.

## What They Learn

Approaches to learning development skills: Play is central to young children's learning and, depending on a child's age and stage of development, the type of play the child engages in will often fall into one or two distinct categories. One type of play that occupies much of a toddler's time is constructive play, which refers to building and creating. Constructive play involves manipulating objects with the goal of creating something new or imagined. The second type of play that preschoolers and schoolagers enjoy involves an element of pretend or make-believe. Referred to as symbolic play, it occurs when children use one thing to represent another—for example, pretending to talk to someone on a toy phone or baking a cake in a toy oven.

## Extending the Learning

By watching and listening to how children play with the watercraft, you can fairly easily determine the category of their play. Toddlers engaged in constructive play will enjoy exploring how a material floats. They may try to load up their watercraft with as many objects as they can before it sinks or tips over. Preschoolers engaged in dramatic play with their watercraft might pretend that toy people are fishing from the boats in a stormy sea, and schoolagers might use theirs to dramatize everything from the sinking of the *Titanic* to a whitewater rafting vacation.

## What You Need

☐ a variety of lightweight trays and containers (such as those used for fruit, sandwiches, and eggs)

☐ assorted trim items (spools, cord, and pipe cleaners, for example)

☐ scissors

☐ waterproof glue

☐ small, heavy objects (such as flat rocks)

☐ string

## How to Make It

1. Be creative! For the base, choose a container that best suits what you plan to make. Then glue other containers or other items to the base, outfitting it as you see fit. This is a great project for schoolagers to do on their own.

2. To stabilize the craft, glue a small object in the center of the bottom of it.

3. If you're going to launch the craft outside on puddles or rivulets, tie a string to the craft so the children can guide it.

Create an environmentally friendly boat dramatic play area by cutting a large appliance box in half to make two boats. Place the boats on top of an old blue sheet, or have the children paint a water mural. The children can make the fish on page 84, then have fun fishing.

GREEN IDEA • GREEN IDEA

# Backpack and Sit-Upon

## Who

Preschoolers and schoolagers

## About the Toy

These inexpensive and practical props encourage creative play and outdoor exploration. Wearing their own backpacks on walks provides opportunities for children to learn about being responsible for their own possessions. The backpacks and sit-upons can enhance real nature experiences as well as encourage classroom discussion about different kinds of outdoor exploration, such as camping, hiking, and climbing mountains.

## What They Learn

Approaches to learning development skills: Recent research indicates that exposure to nature is essential for healthy childhood development, both physically and emotionally. In fact, some studies show that the absence of nature in the lives of today's children can be linked to some of the most trou-blesome trends of the past few years, such as childhood obesity, attention disorders, and depression. (Louv, R. *Last Child in the Woods: Saving Our Children from Nature-Deficit Disorder*. Chapel Hill, NC: Algonquin Books, 2008.)

## Extending the Learning

Preschoolers and schoolagers will enjoy using these backpacks and sit-upons to enhance a variety of outdoor experiences. For example, children can use the backpacks to carry lightweight objects and natural treasures found on walks outdoors. By using the backpacks to collect litter, such as pop cans, bottles, and trash, they learn the importance of taking care of the environment. The sit-upons make sitting outdoors more comfortable, whether on a nature hike, at a picnic, or listening to a story outdoors.

## What You Need

**BACKPACK:**

☐ one large grocery bag per child (two bags per child if you want the backpacks to be extra sturdy)

☐ one manila envelope per child

☐ two business-size envelopes per child

☐ glue

☐ markers and other materials for decorating the backpacks

☐ two tagboard strips or other suitable material (1½ by 24 inches per child)

☐ masking tape or duct tape

- ☐ scissors
- ☐ stapler
- ☐ cards with children's names and emergency phone numbers

## SIT-UPON:

- ☐ old newspapers, Styrofoam pellets, or other light stuffing material
- ☐ two large heavy-duty resealable plastic bags per child
- ☐ sharp pin
- ☐ masking tape or duct tape

# How to Make It

## BACKPACK

1. If you are using two bags, fit one inside the other. Fold in 2 or 3 inches of the edge.

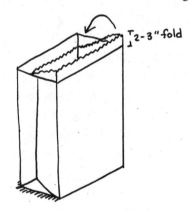

2. Glue the manila envelope to the front of the backpack. Make sure to leave one end of each envelope open. Glue the business-size envelopes to the sides of the bag.

3. Let the children decorate their backpacks.

4. Staple one end of the tagboard strips near the center of the backpack's top. Staple the other ends near the outside edges at the bottom of the backpack. Reinforce with tape. Make sure the straps fit in a way that allows the child to easily put on and take off the backpack.

## SIT-UPON

1. Shred newspapers (children love this part) or prepare other stuffing materials. Put the material into one plastic bag until the bag is plump. Make small holes (pinprick size) in the corners of the bag to release air.

2. Zip the bag shut and slip the other bag over it so the zippers are at opposite ends. Zip the second bag shut. Reinforce with tape for extra durability. Repeat the air removal procedure for the second bag.

Take a walk and clean up your yard or neighborhood. Line the backpacks with plastic grocery bags. Have children walk in pairs so one child can collect trash while the other collects recyclable cans and bottles. Be sure the children wear gloves and wash their hands after handling trash. When cleaning up a neighborhood park or playground, do the collecting on the return walk.

# Very Kool Playdough

## Who

Toddlers, preschoolers, and schoolagers

## About the Toy

Most children enjoy rolling, kneading, patting, shaping, cutting, and poking playdough. They use it to create everything from cookies to creatures. Making the playdough helps older children learn to measure, mix, read a recipe, and follow directions. Using the playdough enhances children's creativity, provides practice in using hands and fingers to control and manipulate materials, and offers a soothing, relaxing sensory experience. To enhance children's play, be sure to supply them with sculpting tools and other props such as round blocks or rolling pins, cookie cutters, and molds. Mixing playdough of different colors teaches color identification and how to make colors.

## What They Learn

Cognitive development skills: *Scaffolding* is a term familiar to early childhood educators; it means changing the level of support or guidance during a learning experience based on the child's needs. For example, when a young child is learning a new task, an adult working with the child may at first use primarily direct instruction. As children learn a task, they need less and less guidance. Involving children in following basic recipes, such as this one for playdough, creates situations in which scaffolding will likely occur.

## Extending the Learning

Cooking activities present many opportunities for learning. Even though most toddlers and preschoolers cannot read, they still learn about measuring and measurement vocabulary. Toddlers and preschoolers are not likely to grasp the concept of quantities, but allowing them to play with and manipulate measuring tools establishes a foundation for future understanding. Schoolagers can be expected to follow the directions and measure out the appropriate amounts. Use your knowledge of the children you are working with to help you determine how much guidance to give them.

## What You Need

- ☐ 2½ cups flour
- ☐ ½ cup salt
- ☐ 1 Tbsp. alum (found in the spice section of most grocery stores)
- ☐ two envelopes unsweetened drink mix
- ☐ 3 Tbsp. cooking oil
- ☐ 2 cups boiling water
- ☐ covered plastic container or resealable plastic bag

## How to Make It

1. In a large bowl, mix together the flour, salt, alum, and drink mix. Add the oil and the boiling water to the dry ingredients. Mix well.

2. When the mixture is cool enough to handle, knead it until it is well mixed, then let it cool.

3. Between uses, store the playdough in the refrigerator in the covered container or a resealable plastic bag.

## Variation

Use different flavors (and colors) of drink mix to vary the smell and look of the playdough.

Homemade playdough requires minimal packaging. If you use large, clean yogurt tubs or plastic ice cream containers you will save money and energy by reusing something that otherwise would end up in a landfill.

GREEN IDEA • GREEN IDEA

# Fancy Fish

## Who

Toddlers, preschoolers, and schoolagers

## About the Toy

These fancy fish toys can be used in fun craft activities to teach children about tropical fish and ocean life by illustrating the shape and characteristics of real fish. Before the children make their own, show them pictures of fish. Discuss with them where fish live and the body parts of fish, including their bright colors, the shapes of their tails, and the placement of their eyes. Decorate the room with the fish, create a tropical fish display, or use the fish in dramatic play about fishing, snorkeling, or scuba diving. For another fun activity, attach magnets to the fish and invite children to fish for them using homemade fishing poles.

## What They Learn

Physical and motor development skills: Compared to when they were infants, children between ages two and five are much more physically developed and skilled. Their fine-motor skills now include the ability to pour from a pitcher, use eating utensils, button buttons, build block towers, string large beads, put together puzzles, cut with scissors, and scribble on paper. What a long way they've come!

## Extending the Learning

Provide children with a variety of craft items and writing and drawing tools, and encourage them to decorate their fish in any way they choose. As they create, watch how they use the various materials and tools. Comment on their fish creations, recognizing that it is the process of creating that is most important, not the final product: "Wow! Look at all those stripes on your fish!" "You used three stickers to decorate your fish. Now what will you use?"

## What You Need

- ☐ small paper bags or shiny Mylar bags from snack packs
- ☐ glue stick
- ☐ coding dots or stickers
- ☐ markers and crayons
- ☐ scissors
- ☐ newspaper
- ☐ yarn
- ☐ strip magnet, large metal bolt, and long pole or stick (optional)

## How to Make It

1. Lay the bag flat. Fold the closed corners toward the center of the bag and glue them to form a fish shape.

2. Decorate both sides of the bag using markers or crayons. Stick coding dots on each side for

eyes. Optional: Use scissors to fringe the open edge of the bag.

3. Have the children shred newspaper and stuff it into the bags. Do not overstuff. Using the yarn, tie off the end 2 inches from the tail.

4. For a fishing activity, glue a 1-inch piece of strip magnet to the side of the fish. Tie a metal bolt to one end of a length of yarn, and attach the other end of the yarn to the pole or stick for a homemade fishing pole. (Keep the string very short for young children and beginners. Lengthen the string as their abilities grow.)

If you live near a body of water, help keep it clean by preventing plastic bags from entering the water. Plastic bags can harm wildlife.

GREEN IDEA • GREEN IDEA

# Portable Easels

## Who

Toddlers, preschoolers, and schoolagers

## About the Toy

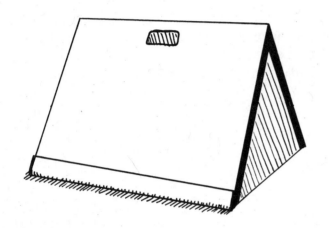

You can easily make enough of these inexpensive, easy-to-store easels so that a small group of children can paint at the same time. Having a number of easels on hand is especially important when toddlers are involved because it is difficult for them to wait for their turn. These easels facilitate spontaneous use of art materials because children can set up a painting project whenever and wherever they feel like it. The easels also teach children to be resourceful and encourage them to be responsible for their art materials.

## What They Learn

Approaches to learning development skills: Young children's drawings and paintings contain simple lines and irregular contours, which result in figures that lack proportion, often in bright, unmixed colors. Despite their lack of realism, they are appealing because of what they suggest: freedom, spontaneity, directness, innocence, and even humor.

## Extending the Learning

For many children, art is an important way of conveying their feelings and ideas, some of which they are not yet capable of expressing in words. Not all children embrace art with enthusiasm, however. While it is important to make available materials such as these portable easels that encourage artistic expression, keep in mind that not all children will be inspired to create with them. Your knowledge of a child's preferences will help you tailor her learning experiences, artistic or otherwise, to fit her preferences.

## What You Need

- ☐ large, sturdy square cardboard box (about 20 inches per side)
- ☐ oil cloth or other waterproof material
- ☐ utility knife
- ☐ pencil
- ☐ ruler or yardstick
- ☐ stapler or duct tape
- ☐ scissors
- ☐ clothespins or large paper clips
- ☐ Velcro
- ☐ six-pack of juice cartons for paints

## How to Make It

1. Place the box bottom up. Cut it apart along one bottom edge, from corner to corner. Draw

a line and cut diagonally from the cut corner to the opposite corner on two sides. Trim off the flap from the top of the box.

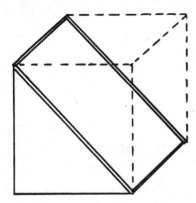

*Note:* Two easels can be made from one box if the top can be taped shut. Then, instead of cutting the flap off, you end up with a second easel.

2. Cut a 2-inch slot out of each side of the top edge of the easel.

3. For the waterproof covering, measure the width of the easel and the overall length, and then cut out a section of oil cloth that is 4 inches larger. Fold up 2 inches of each end and staple or tape it along the side (this creates

pockets to contain paint drippings). Drape the cloth over the easel and cut out 2-inch slots at the top to match the ones in the cardboard. Attach a clothespin or paper clip in each slot on each side.

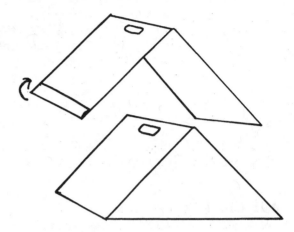

4. On the inside of the easel, attach 2- to 4-inch strips of Velcro, side by side, about 2 inches apart. Lay clean brushes across the strips and lay the corresponding Velcro strips over the brushes. (See the Art-and-Writing-Tool Holder, p. 88, for brush storage alternatives.)

5. Cover the outside of the juice cartons with oil cloth to reinforce them for carrying paints.

Reusing a material is best for the environment. When you have finished using a reusable material, be sure to recycle it if possible.

GREEN IDEA · GREEN IDEA

# Art-and-Writing-Tool Holder

## Who

Toddlers, preschoolers, and schoolagers

## About the Toy

Children can keep many tools in these tool holders. Large coffee cans should hold ten or more scissors or paintbrushes. Small cans can hold one to two of each or one pair of scissors and one paintbrush. Children can each have their own tool holder, which encourages them to be responsible for the tools they use. Have children return scissors and other tools to the slots when not in use, and emphasize to them that they should always place the tools point side down in the holders. For groups sharing tool holders, use two medium-size cans and spread out the cans at a worktable for easy use.

## What They Learn

Social and emotional development skills: Self-efficacy is the belief that one can master a situation and produce a favorable outcome; it is the belief that "I can." As children grow and mature, they are able to do more and more things for themselves. Child development theorists, such as Albert Bandura, believe self-efficacy is a key factor in whether or not a child achieves in school. Not surprisingly, self-efficacy also plays a role in shaping a child's self-concept and self-esteem.

## Extending the Learning

Activities that challenge young children but also allow them to achieve some degree of success are the kinds of activities most likely to fully engage children. These tool holders provide a safe way for children to carry and learn to take proper care of scissors and other tools. The holders also can foster neatness, organizational skills, and responsibility for materials as well as self-directed activities using scissors. When you entrust a child to take care of materials such as scissors and other everyday tools, you are sending the message "You can."

## What You Need

☐ coffee can or other can with a plastic lid

☐ contact paper or other decorative covering

☐ markers

☐ utility knife

## How to Make It

1. Cover the can with the contact paper or another covering. When suitable, let the children help decorate the can.

2. Place the plastic lid on the can. Use the utility knife to make suitable holes for paintbrushes, rulers, and other tools.

## Variation

To create a small puppet holder, place dowels that are 4 inches longer than the can into the holes.

Save water when cleaning food containers by placing them all in the sink and filling just one with water. Use a scrub brush to loosen stuck food, then pour the water into another container.

GREEN IDEA · GREEN IDEA

# Paper-Bag Balls

## Who

Toddlers, preschoolers, and schoolagers

## About the Toy

Use these balls outdoors or in a large, open area indoors. Children will find these balls easy to use for practicing kicking, throwing, and batting. Toddlers may enjoy dropping and tossing the balls into large laundry baskets or boxes. Preschoolers and schoolagers can make their own balls and work in pairs to kick or toss the balls back and forth. To encourage cooperative play, create simple team games using walls or trees as goals, or establish an obstacle course and have the children kick balls through the course from beginning to end.

## What They Learn

Physical and motor development skills: Among the gross-motor skills children of this age practice and refine are ball-handling skills, that is, games and activities involving balls. Two- to three-year-old children usually can kick a ball and stand and throw a ball. By the time they are four or five, chil-

dren typically can throw a ball underhanded about four feet, catch a large ball, and catch a bounced ball. Ball-handling skills are important for children to develop—they encourage gross-motor coordination and hand-eye and foot-eye coordination, usually in a fun-filled setting.

## Extending the Learning

Children's motor skills progress in a sequential manner over time, from immature to advanced. Although motor-skill development is seen as age related, it is not necessarily age determined; for example, one four-year-old child may be able to catch a bounced ball, while another child the same age may still be unable to catch a ball tossed lightly from a short distance. Therefore, when playing ball-related games with several children at once, it's important to take note of each child's physical abilities and make any necessary adjustments to the activity to ensure that each child's experiences are successful.

## What You Need

☐ medium-size paper bag

☐ newspapers

☐ markers and crayons

☐ stapler

☐ duct tape

## How to Make It

1. Write the child's name in the center of the bag and let each child decorate his or her own bag for easy identification.

2. Ask the children to tear lots of newspapers into strips or pieces.

3. Stuff the newspaper into the bag until it is about three-fourths full. Mold the bag so it forms a round shape.

4. Fold over the top of the bag and staple it shut. Cover the stapled section with tape to reinforce the closure.

## Variation

Make smaller balls out of wadded-up newspaper formed into a round shape and covered with duct tape.

After the balls have been played with and are starting to fall apart, recycle them!

GREEN IDEA · GREEN IDEA ·

# Paddle Ball

## Who

Toddlers, preschoolers, and schoolagers

## About the Toy

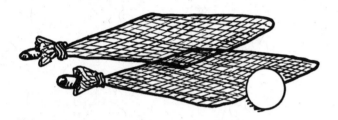

These paddle balls encourage outdoor physical play and require only free and easily found portable materials. Younger children will use the paddles in individual play, pushing lightweight, medium-size balls around as if putting a golf ball. You can also place a box on its side for children to use as a goal to aim at, which helps build large-muscle control. Older children will be able to use the paddles in more sophisticated activities, such as batting the ball over and over and counting to see how long they can keep it up. Older children may find it challenging to put together a miniature golf course using items such as carpet samples, three-pound coffee cans with both ends removed, and strategically placed blocks. Old tennis balls can be used on the course as well.

## What They Learn

Physical and motor development skills: Children between the ages of two and five are very active. Toddlers and preschoolers enjoy simple movements such as hopping, jumping, and running just for the sheer delight of performing these activities. In fact, three-year-old children have the highest activity level of any age in the entire human life span! Using equipment such as these paddle balls, requires coordinated movements and challenges this age group to further develop both fine-motor and gross-motor skills.

## Extending the Learning

By regularly observing the physical skills of a child, you gain a clearer picture of his development, which you can use to determine adjustments that may need to be made to best meet his ability level. This kind of individualized instruction may also play a role in shaping his enthusiasm for and interest in physical activities as he grows. If a child is active throughout his childhood and teen years, it is likely he will lead an active lifestyle as an adult as well.

## What You Need

### FOR EACH PADDLE:

☐ one heavy-duty wire hanger

☐ pliers

☐ duct tape

☐ one clean pair of panty hose (for a sturdier and longer-lasting paddle, use knit tights or two leg portions of panty hose per paddle)

☐ rubber band

☐ scissors

☐ variety of small- to medium-size balls (such as Nerf, pom-poms, tennis balls, badminton birdies, crumpled newspaper balls, balloons, and whiffle or Ping-Pong balls)

☐ large cardboard box (optional)

## How to Make It

1. Bend the hanger into a round or diamond shape. To create a handle, use pliers to bend down the hook of the hanger and twist it snuggly around its base. Cover the handle with duct tape.

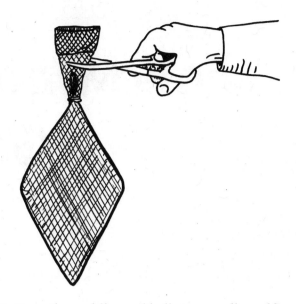

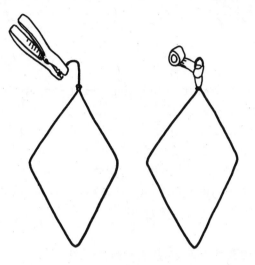

2. Slip the leg portion of the panty hose over the hanger. Wrap a rubber band over the handle to keep the stocking ends tightly in place. Cut off the excess panty hose and retape with additional duct tape.

3. Store the paddles and balls in a cardboard box.

## Variation

Create a miniature golf course. Make various obstacles out of old rugs or carpet samples and large coffee cans or plastic buckets with the bottoms cut out. Use large pieces of Mylar or aluminum foil to represent water traps. Gather old tennis balls and encourage the children to putt through the course.

Ask for donations of old panty hose and knit tights. Use sections that do not have runs or holes.

GREEN IDEA • GREEN IDEA

# Following-Footsteps Game

## Who

Toddlers, preschoolers, and schoolagers

## About the Toy

These footprints help children refine their balancing skills. Toddlers will simply follow footprints placed at appropriate distances for their stride. For preschoolers, place the feet close enough together so the children can hop or step from one to another. Older preschoolers and schoolagers can work in pairs, taking turns rolling a die and taking the number of steps indicated on the die. They may also count aloud as they step, or they may want to name and match the foot they land on as right or left.

Use the footprints indoors or outdoors. Indoors, use them as paths to activities or to the bathroom, giving children direction while still allowing for and encouraging independence. Outdoors, use the footprints to create longer paths, such as to a back fence or all around the play area.

## What They Learn

Physical and motor development skills: Balancing skills are acquired over time. By the age of three, most children can balance momentarily on one foot. By the time they are five, they are able to walk along a line on the floor, walk forward and backward heel to toe, and run on their tiptoes. Games that incorporate novel props and new challenges, such as this Following-Footsteps Game, foster balancing skills in fun ways that are appropriate for all children in this age group.

## Extending the Learning

Although the aim of this game is to help children refine balancing skills, don't be surprised if toddlers would rather pick up the footprints than follow them around the room. Let them do what is important to them now. For older children, the game encourages social development through playing with others and taking turns. Following the random zigzag paths of the footprints also enhances older children's concepts of position and direction, for example, left and right.

## What You Need

☐ paper for tracing

☐ pencil

☐ child's foot or shoe

☐ wallpaper samples, thin rug samples, or any material that will lie flat on the floor

☐ scissors

☐ die

☐ good pictures of animal tracks

## How to Make It

1. With a pencil, trace a child's right and left foot on a piece of tracing paper.

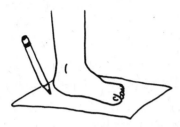

2. Cut the footprints from the tracing paper. Using the tracings as a pattern, cut the number of feet appropriate for your space and purpose from the chosen materials.

3. Make your own die, following the directions on page 204.

## Variations

Make feet measuring tapes by taping or paper-clipping footprints together (toe to heel). Let the children use the measuring tape to measure things around the room.

If the material you used to make the footprints has a variety of different patterns, mount samples of those patterns on index cards. Have children pick a card and go to a footprint that corresponds to the pattern.

Instead of children's footprints, create animal prints with the children's help (make them larger than life-size). Children can follow the animal prints and pretend to go on a safari in search of the animal.

Create and maintain a file folder of tracings. That way you won't waste paper re-creating a tracing each time you need a pattern.

# Workout Weights

## Who

Toddlers, preschoolers, and schoolagers

## About the Toy

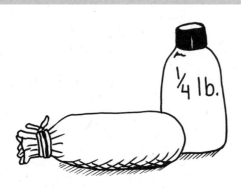

Working out with weights helps children learn to enjoy using their bodies, alone or with a group, and encourages a lifelong interest in taking care of themselves. You and the children can do upper-body workouts together using weights appropriate to each person's size, ability, and strength. By customizing the weights to each child's ability and strength, all children can participate and succeed.

Let the children choose weights that are comfortable and appropriate for them. For toddlers, the weights should be very light—no heavier than about ¼ pound. Preschoolers and schoolagers can do specific exercises with the weights that focus on different muscle groups, whereas toddlers will simply enjoy holding the weights and moving their bodies in fun ways. Consider playing a CD with an upbeat tempo while you and the children work out with the weights.

Children should use the weights only for as long as they find it fun and challenging. Before doing any exercise, children and adults should warm up their muscles through stretching exercises.

## What They Learn

Physical and motor development skills: Achieving lifelong health and fitness begins with healthy habits acquired during the childhood years. Working out with weights introduces children to the concepts of personal health and fitness, such as learning about their bodies (muscles), warming up muscles before exercising, and developing upper-body strength.

## Extending the Learning

What kinds of vocabulary are children using when they use the weights? Do they express enjoyment of the physical activities? When you show enthusiasm about and pleasure in movement and fitness, you are helping foster the same kind of enthusiasm in the children.

## What You Need

- ☐ old and mismatched socks, sleeves from old shirts, or small plastic bottles with secure screw-top covers
- ☐ plastic bread bags
- ☐ sand or water
- ☐ cord or string
- ☐ scissors
- ☐ duct tape
- ☐ scale

# How to Make It

## SOCK OR SLEEVE WEIGHT

1. Choose appropriate-sized socks or cut sections of shirt sleeves. If using a sleeve, tie off one open end.

2. Fill the bread bag with clean sand. Set the scale in the area you will use to assemble the weights. Invite schoolage children to help you weigh the weights as they are constructed. Assist the children with reading the scale, if needed. Use ¼ pound—same as a stick of butter—for toddlers, and up to 3 or 4 pounds for adults. Fill the weight loosely enough so that the children can easily grip the center. Have the schoolage children help keep track of the weights by putting them in piles by weight.

3. Tie off the bag with string. Slip the bag of sand into the sock or sleeve and securely tie off the open end.

## PLASTIC BOTTLE WEIGHT

1. Fill a small bottle with sand or water to the desired weight.

2. Screw on the cover and secure it with duct tape.

3. Invite older children to write the size of the weights on the bottles. Assist children with writing, if needed.

When the children are finished with the weights, empty the socks or bottles and reuse them again for something else. See the Reusable and Donated Materials Index on page 221 for ideas.

GREEN IDEA • GREEN IDEA •

# Bottle Drop

## Who

Toddlers, preschoolers, and schoolagers

## About the Toy

This game can be played indoors or outdoors and can be easily adapted to each child's skill level. For younger children, you may need to model standing over a bottle and dropping rings over it.

Older children can form teams, keep track of scores, and make up rules for the game.

## What They Learn

Physical and motor development skills: Simple ring-toss games such as this one help young children develop hand-eye coordination and provide practice in judging distance, position, and direction—all useful perceptual-motor skills.

## Extending the Learning

Games such as ring toss require the development of more specific physical skills, such as the ability to gauge how hard and how far to toss a ring to make it go over the neck of the bottle. Your knowledge of a child's abilities in these areas will enable you to set up activities that are appropriate as well as challenging and fun. While a young toddler might only be interested in slipping the rings on and off the bottle, a schoolager might enjoy being challenged to toss the rings over the neck of the bottle from farther and farther away as well as keep track of the number of "ringers" she makes.

## What You Need

☐ 2-liter plastic bottle with cap

☐ funnel and scoop

☐ sand or water

☐ superglue

☐ strong tape

☐ heavy piece of plastic (such as a shower curtain, plastic tablecloth, or tarp)

☐ yardstick

☐ permanent marker

☐ pencil

☐ string

☐ hoops (plastic bracelets, large drapery rings, rings from rolls of tape, or canning rings)

## How to Make It

1. Wash the bottle thoroughly and let it dry. Using a funnel and scoop, fill the bottle with about 2 inches of sand or water to help stabilize it.

2. Glue the cap securely on and cover it with strong tape.

3. For the target circles, lay the plastic sheet on a flat surface and place the bottle in the center. Trace around it with a marker. This is the bull's eye. To draw the other circles, tie one end of a piece of string to a pencil. With one person holding the pencil securely in the bull's eye, a second person can mark every 8 to 10 inches from the center of the circle by tying the marker to the string and drawing perfectly round circles.

Instead of purchasing a commercial toy-bowling product, use smaller bottles to make a bowling game. Use a rubber or plastic ball. Children can make up their own scoring system by assigning point values to the pins.

GREEN IDEA · GREEN IDEA ·

# Child-Size Game Net

## Who

Toddlers, preschoolers, and schoolagers

## About the Toy

This net encourages cooperative play with others. It introduces simplified game-playing concepts, rules, and techniques such as throwing balls over and under a net, rolling balls under a net, and bouncing and batting balls with hands or a paddle. The net can be used indoors or outdoors, and it can be adjusted to children's interests, sizes, and throwing abilities. Begin with the net at or slightly above the children's height. Indoors, string the net between two doorknobs, chairs, or railings. Outdoors, string the net between two trees or posts. Be sure there is an open playing area on either side of the net that is free of objects children could trip over.

Two or more children can throw or bat balls back and forth over the net. Large, soft balls, such as Nerf balls or beach balls, work best. For batting, use badminton birdies, yarn balls, or newspaper balls (see Paper-Bag Balls, p. 90).

## What They Learn

Social and emotional development skills: The ability to manage their emotions helps children get along with one another. Toddlers and some preschoolers are still learning impulse control and will continue to need many opportunities to practice mastering this behavior. In addition, their limited language skills make it more difficult for them to express themselves using words. Older preschoolers and schoolagers, however, are better at managing their emotions and also can recognize the feelings of others and respond appropriately. In addition, they are better able to work together to come up with solutions on their own if conflicts arise, which further strengthens their social skills.

## Extending the Learning

When we model behaviors for children, we act the way we want them to behave so they can learn by observing our actions. For example, when helping a child put away toys say, "Please hand me that block." Over time, the child will begin to imitate your polite behavior. When playing a game, model cooperation by saying, "You two can practice hitting over the net first, and then I'll take a turn."

## What You Need

### FOR A 10-FOOT SPACE:

☐ 3 yards of wide elastic material for the net frame

☐ material for the net (such as an old bedsheet)

☐ scissors

☐ yardstick

## How to Make It

1. Cut or tear sixty streamers (each about 30 inches long by 1 to 1½ inches wide) from a bedsheet or other material.

2. Starting at the center of the elastic, tie the streamers to the elastic so at least 2 feet of streamers hang down and there is about ½ inch between each. Leave enough space at each end of the elastic for tying it around trees, posts, or doorknobs.

Ask for donations or visit your local thrift store for old sheets.

GREEN IDEA · GREEN IDEA ·

# A Nesting Ball for the Birds

## Who

Toddlers, preschoolers, and schoolagers

## About the Toy

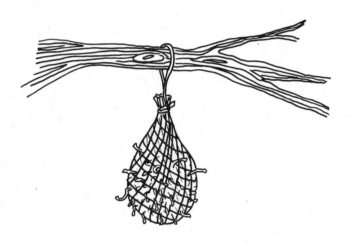

As children see birds fly to and from the nesting ball, they will be introduced to the concept of flight as another means of locomotion. For older children, reading and writing about topics such as flight or birds develops language skills and may inspire lifetime occupations or hobbies such as becoming a pilot, a biologist, or an avid birdwatcher.

## What They Learn

Approaches to learning development skills: Children are fascinated with nature, and in a way, nature is the ultimate classroom. Regular opportunities to explore the natural world help satisfy children's endless curiosity about things. Through careful observations of nature, children learn to appreciate the environment. In turn, they seek out things they can do to preserve and protect our amazing natural world.

## Extending the Learning

Even simple outdoor activities, such as watching and talking about birds or observing and commenting on the wind, will capture a toddler's attention. These are ideal opportunities to enhance his language skills, too, as you ask him to tell you what the birds are doing or how the wind feels on his face. Older children can help you gather the nesting materials, and they will enjoy watching the birds discover the nesting materials, pick at them, and fly off to build their nests. Afterward, be sure to build on the children's learning by offering picture books (for toddlers) or informational books (for preschoolers and schoolagers) featuring birds, fledglings, and nests.

## What You Need

- ☐ nest-building materials (bits of yarn, ribbon, string, dog hair brushings, or lint from a clothes dryer)
- ☐ mesh bag (such as an onion bag)
- ☐ string

## How to Make It

1. Have children collect suitable nesting materials.

2. Stuff the nesting materials into the mesh bag. Tie the bag closed with string.

3. Use the string to hang the ball from a tree branch or other structure that is within easy sight of the children and where the birds can pick at it.

With the children, plant native flowering plants and grasses. Native plants require very little watering and should attract birds, butterflies, and perhaps bees.

GREEN IDEA · GREEN IDEA ·

# Bottle Bird Feeder

## Who

Toddlers, preschoolers, and schoolagers

## About the Toy

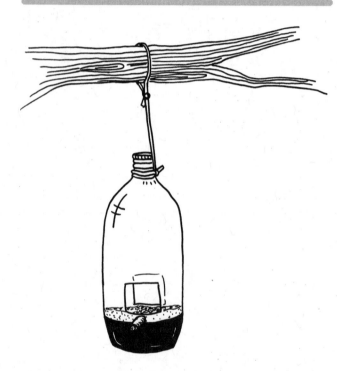

This activity involving a bird feeder promotes children's interest in nature. Children also learn how other creatures eat differently from humans and from one another. Helping make the bird feeders enhances children's small-muscle skills and hand-eye coordination.

## What They Learn

Social and emotional development skills: Activities that promote children's interest in nature serve to strengthen their attachments to the natural world. In addition, activities such as helping to make this

bottle bird feeder teach children the importance of caring for and helping preserve wildlife. These are invaluable lessons for children of any age.

## Extending the Learning

Your knowledge of a child's abilities will help you determine how much she can participate in making the bird feeder. Even if she is too young to help make the feeder, she can watch as you prepare the feeder and will benefit from hearing you describe the process. For example, "I've washed and dried the bottle; now I will mark where to cut the openings so the birds can stick their beaks in and reach the birdseed." Older children can help make the feeder and will enjoy filling it with seeds. So that everyone gets the most from this learning experience, involve all of the children as much as possible in the process.

## What You Need

☐ plastic 2-liter bottle with a cap

☐ permanent marker

☐ utility knife

☐ scissors

☐ strong cord or string (24 inches minimum)

☐ birdseed

☐ dowel (optional)

## How to Make It

1. Have the children wash and dry the bottle.

2. With the marker, draw an outline of two openings 2 inches up from the bottom on opposite

sides of the bottle; openings should be about 2 inches tall and 2 inches wide. With the utility knife, start to cut along each of the lines. Let the children use scissors to complete the openings. Dry the inside of the bottle.

3. If desired, cut two holes the size of the wooden dowel below the feeder opening and insert the dowel through the openings to act as a perch for the birds.

4. Tie the string securely around the neck of the bottle. Fill the bottle with birdseed and hang it where it will be visible, from a window if possible.

Talk with the children about how using recycled materials is a way of protecting the environment in which wild creatures live.

# Preschoolers

# Letter Lineup

## Who

Preschoolers

## About the Toy

This game helps children become familiar with letters by playing with them and matching them up. It also encourages them to become more aware of letters in their environment. Children can play the game individually or as a small group, with each child taking a turn picking a letter to match. If desired, include more than one match for each letter.

## What They Learn

Language and communication development skills: Letter recognition is an important prereading skill and one that is appropriate to introduce to most preschoolers. Games such as this one help preschoolers become familiar with the shapes of letters by noticing their similarities and differences. The variation (on p. 109) can help older preschoolers with initial sound recognition and word-letter associations, both essential prereading skills as well.

## Extending the Learning

As a child works to match individual letters to the letters on the file folders, encourage him to tell you what he knows about each letter by saying, for example, "This letter makes the /k/ sound and is also the first letter in your name. What is this letter called? My name begins with the same letter. *K* is for Kathy." To extend this game, ask the child to point out the same letter in the environment. "I'll bet we can find other *K*'s in the room. Let's go look."

## What You Need

- ☐ construction paper
- ☐ scissors
- ☐ file folders
- ☐ glue stick
- ☐ clear contact paper
- ☐ plastic bag

## How to Make It

1. Trace the letters of the alphabet on construction paper or use preprinted letters that appear on wrapping paper or in magazines. Cut out

the letters. Make sure you have an identical pair of each letter.

2. Glue one letter from each set to the inside of a file folder in random fashion (for young children, use only a few letters). Cover the inside of the folder with clear contact paper.

3. Spread out another piece of contact paper, with the sticky side up. Place all remaining letters on the contact paper. Cover with another piece of contact paper to enclose the letters.

4. Cut out the letters from the contact paper, including the internal parts of letters (where it can be done easily), and match them with the letters on the file folder. When they are not in use, store the letters in the plastic bag.

## Variation

For older children, add a set of cue cards with pictures on them. Have the children match the card to the letter associated with the initial sound of the object pictured (for example, ball matched to the letter *b*). Have children think of words that begin with specific letter sounds.

Ask personnel at local office buildings for donations of used file folders.

GREEN IDEA · GREEN IDEA ·

# Wrapping Paper Match-Ups

## Who

Preschoolers

## About the Toy

This game helps children recognize likenesses and differences and learn about ways of classifying things. It helps the development of language and thinking skills as well as the ability to listen and follow directions. Make each game relate to as many topics as possible. Images of all types of animals, toys, vehicles, flowers, rocket ships, desserts, or school or party scenes are available on wrapping paper, wallpaper, and patterned contact paper.

## What They Learn

Cognitive development skills: Matching activities encourage children to recognize "what is the same" and "what is different" as a way of classify-ing things. A basic thinking skill, matching lays the foundation for the development of other thinking skills, such as the ability to classify and interpret data. Preschoolers who have mastered these skills can then help create simple graphs that represent the data they collect.

## Extending the Learning

If you use this game as a small-group activity for older preschoolers, place the master playing board in the center of the group and give each child in the group several pictures. Ask children questions about the pictures such as, "Who has the picture of the animal that barks?" or "Who has the picture of the animal that wags its tail when it's happy?" The questioning process helps children learn about the different ways information can be organized into logical groupings. As an extension for older pre-schoolers, consider having children create ques-tions using their own criteria, such as "Who has the picture of an animal with wings?"

## What You Need

☐ two sets of patterns found on wrapping paper, wallpaper, or patterned contact paper

☐ scissors

☐ tagboard

☐ glue

☐ clear contact paper

☐ large envelope or plastic bag

☐ paper clip or tape

## How to Make It

1. Cut out two complete sets of all the pictures. Having eight or nine different pictures works best. Glue one set of the pictures to a piece of tagboard. Glue the other set to another piece of tagboard.

2. Cover both boards with the contact paper.

3. For playing pieces, cut out the individual pictures from one of the boards. Leave the other board whole to use as the playing board.

4. When not in use, store the pieces in an envelope or plastic bag. Paper clip or tape the envelope to the playing board.

Ask at local art or office supply stores for donations of tagboard. They may have slightly damaged tagboard sheets that they cannot sell but that would be perfectly fine for you to use.

GREEN IDEA · GREEN IDEA

# Look-Alikes

## Who

Preschoolers

## About the Toy

To play this game, children complete each row with pictures that match. One or two children can play. Place all of the cards face down on a table. Children then take turns picking a card and finding its match on the playing board. Play continues until all of the cards are used and rows are complete.

## What They Learn

Language and communication development skills: Prereading skills are an essential part of learning to read. Included among these skills is print awareness, that is, knowledge about print and its conventions and functions, such as recognizing that print is read from left to right. Children are practicing this skill in this game as they work to match the pictures from left to right. In addition, the game helps develop a child's concentration, memory, and persistence in completing a task—all of which contribute to her becoming a comfortable and competent reader.

## Extending the Learning

This game can be extended to help a preschooler's development in other areas, such as visual discrimination skills involving paying attention to details. If the game is not challenging enough for a child, you can make it more challenging by using stickers or wrapping-paper pictures that are smaller and more similar. Do not be tempted, however, to use the game as a patterning activity for children this age, since most games involving extending and creating patterns are more appropriate for four- and five-year-olds.

## What You Need

☐ wrapping paper or stickers

☐ scissors

☐ ruler

☐ marker

☐ glue

☐ index cards (5 by 8 inches)

☐ clear contact paper

## How to Make It

1. Cut out three sets of each pattern or design from the wrapping paper or use three sets of stickers.

2. To make the playing board, draw lines on the file cards, making squares the size required for the pictures or stickers. Glue a picture or a sticker in the first box of each row. Cover with clear contact paper.

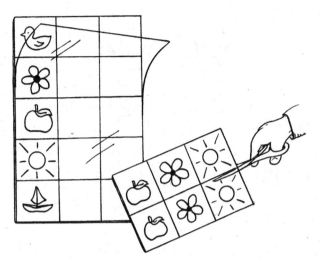

3. To make the game pieces, mount the remaining pictures or stickers onto file cards. Cover with contact paper. Cut out the pictures or stickers in individual squares that will fit the boxes on the playing board. Suitable stickers would be ones that are similar to one another, such as various types of butterflies or fish, decorated hearts, or flowers.

## Variations

Encourage the children to use the cards to play a game like Old Maid. They can pick cards from one another to make pairs.

Have the children lay out the cards, face down, and play a game of concentration, as described in Picture Partners (see p. 140).

Reuse wrapping paper for this game. Suitable paper contains small pattern prints that are similar in size but slightly different in some way (for example, different in color or pattern). Wrapping paper with five or more different images (as opposed to designs) works best. For example, wrapping-paper images might include small toys in boxes; hearts and flowers in a squared-off design format; and rows of small trucks, animals, clothes, or snowmen.

GREEN IDEA • GREEN IDEA

# Shape Finders

## Who

Preschoolers

## About the Toy

The child finds a small card with the shape on it that completes each sequence and places it in the empty box on the playing card. One child can play as an independent activity, or two to four children may play as a type of bingo game.

## What They Learn

Cognitive development skills: Although young preschoolers cannot create simple patterns on their own, most can recognize a simple sequential pattern and use clues such as shape and color to help solve a problem. This type of activity encourages the development of thinking skills as a child tries to decide what comes next.

## Extending the Learning

While observing a child playing this game, use it as an opportunity to reinforce his language skills by talking with him about the different shapes and colors on the cards. For example, ask him to name and describe the shapes, and ask how they are the same and different: "What is the name of this shape? Yes, it is a circle. Do circles have pointed sides? Which shapes have pointed sides?" Ask her about the shapes' colors too. "What color is this shape? Green. You're right. Is this one green? No, it's not green, it's red. Right again."

## What You Need

☐ unlined index cards (5 by 8 inches)

☐ stickers or colored coding dots

☐ marker

☐ clear contact paper

☐ Velcro

☐ scissors

☐ business-size envelope

## How to Make It

1. On four to six of the index cards, arrange the stickers or dots in four rows, using a different sequence in each row.

2. Draw lines between each row and a box at the end of each row for the answer cards. Cover the cards with clear contact paper. Mount a small piece of Velcro in each answer box.

3. To make the answer cards, draw lines on additional index cards to create small squares that will fit into the answer boxes. Inside each box, mount the sticker or dot that correctly completes the sequence and cover the card with clear contact paper.

4. Cut the answer cards into individual pieces. Mount small pieces of Velcro on the back of the answer cards. Store the pieces in an envelope.

Instead of purchasing a commercial Bingo game, make your own: Make several large game cards and matching cards. Give players one or two of the large game cards. Put all of the smaller pieces in a pile. Children take turns picking the small cards and seeing who has the matching picture on their large card. You may want to serve as a caller or demonstrator the first few times the game is used. Continue playing until all the cards have been completed.

# Sort It!

## Who

Preschoolers

## About the Toy

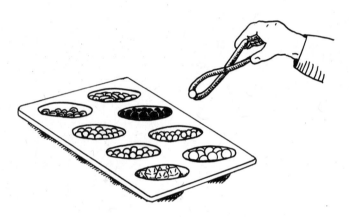

This activity offers a way to use common materials such as beads and buttons to teach specific concepts such as matching colors and shapes. Sorting tasks help children learn to recognize identifying characteristics (likenesses and differences) and then to organize items by various categories.

Put out a muffin tin and a container of small plastic beads. Have children sort the beads into the cups by color, matching the bead color to the cue color circle in each cup. You can change the sorting activity by varying the sorting criteria. For example, liners set in the muffin tin can be made to indicate sorting by quantity (number 1 through 8 in the bottom of the cups), shapes, outlines, or colors of specific items such as buttons. You can vary the activity by adding tweezers or small tongs the children can use to pick up the beads or other items.

## What They Learn

Physical and motor development skills: As soon as a child begins to walk, her hands are suddenly free to work on fine-motor skills, or skills involving small body movements. As with gross-motor skills, fine-motor skills also follow a universal sequence, but they progress according to each child's individual timetable. During the preschool years, some of the fine-motor skills children practice include assembling large puzzles, holding large crayons and paintbrushes, pouring liquids, and cutting with scissors. Activities such as picking up small items with tongs offer great opportunities for preschoolers to practice using the small muscles in their hands.

## Extending the Learning

Manipulating tweezers or tongs will be a fun challenge for most preschoolers, as it requires both hand-eye and small-muscle coordination. If, however, you notice a child who is consistently unable to pick up items with the tool and is becoming frustrated, try switching to larger, softer items, such as large pom-poms, crumpled paper, or wads of play-dough. Then, after the child has mastered picking up those items, reintroduce the original items to the muffin tin.

## What You Need

☐ 6 to 8-cup muffin tin

☐ construction paper

☐ scissors

- ☐ pencil
- ☐ items to sort (such as colored plastic or wooden beads, buttons, counting cubes, beans, pegs, plastic shapes, counting bears, large marbles, lids, or poker chips)
- ☐ tweezers or tongs
- ☐ bowls

## How to Make It

1. Trace the bottom of the muffin tin on colored construction paper that closely matches the colors of the items being sorted. Make one circle from each color.

2. Cut out the circles and place one inside each cup.

3. Fill small bowls with many multicolored beads or other materials to sort.

Used muffin tins can often be found at thrift stores. Be sure there are no rust spots on old metal tins.

# Pizza Pinups

## Who

Preschoolers

## About the Toy

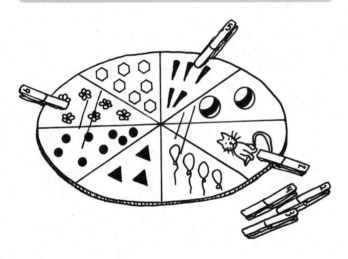

This game helps children learn correct numerical values by giving them practice in counting and matching, and it provides practice with the idea that each number stands for a corresponding quantity. The game also provides an opportunity for a few children to work cooperatively to complete a task and to help one another as needed in identifying the numbers.

Use this game in an activity area that involves numbers or as a small group or individual activity. Tell the children to look at one slice (or section) of the pizza board and count how many pictures they see in it. Have a child find the clothespin with the matching number on it. If the child is not sure of the number, turn over the clothespin and count the dots to see if the numbers match. Then clip that clothespin to the corresponding pizza slice. Continue until all the clothespins are attached.

## What They Learn

Cognitive development skills: *Number and operations* is the term used in early childhood education to indicate certain skills in mathematics. As the name implies, number and operations has to do with numbers and how they are used, for example, connecting number names to the amounts they represent. The best kinds of math-related activities for young children incorporate a variety of learning experiences and allow children to manipulate and come to understand mathematical ideas through their play.

## Extending the Learning

Connecting numbers to the amounts they represent can be a challenging concept for children this age. In fact, it may take some preschoolers a while before they can grasp the idea of clipping the numbered clothespin to the corresponding slice of pizza. If so, simply adjust the game a bit by having children place the corresponding number of small items such as large buttons or wooden beads on the pizza slices instead.

## What You Need

☐ cardboard circles (any size)

☐ small stickers or coding dots

☐ markers

☐ ruler

☐ clip-style clothespins and a container to hold them

☐ clear contact paper

## How to Make It

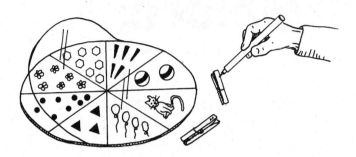

1. Draw dark lines on your cardboard circles, dividing each into eighths.

2. Draw pictures or arrange stickers in each section of the board for quantities from one to eight.

3. Write the numerals 1 to 8 on clothespins. On the opposite side of each clothespin, draw the corresponding number of dots (or use small coding dots).

4. Cover the cardboard circles with clear contact paper. Store the clothespins in a suitable container.

## Variation

Create similar games to match colors or shapes. For older preschoolers or schoolagers, make an identification game using pictures of objects that begin with the same letter in each section of the cardboard circle. Write the corresponding letter on the clothespin.

Using clothespins for what they were originally intended, to hang clothes for drying, saves energy and money, since the sun and wind do the work of your dryer. If you prefer your clothes soft to the touch, place outdoor-dried clothes in your dryer for just a few minutes and let them tumble with no heat.

GREEN IDEA • GREEN IDEA •

# Numbers Galore

## Who

Preschoolers

## About the Toy

Because this game has many possible adaptations, it encourages adults and children to try out new ideas and illustrates how one item can be used in various ways. The game teaches numeral recognition as well as matching like sets and matching numerals to the correct quantity. It encourages counting from one to six and introduces the concept of number sets (four cards each with the number 3 on them are a set of threes). It also encourages playing some games in noncompetitive ways, allowing all players to participate simultaneously. You and the children can also use this game in combination with counters or dice to make other matching or counting games.

You and the children can play numerous games with these sets of cards.

**Noncompetitive Bingo:** Four children each have a bingo board and counters. Call out the number and have the children cover that number with a marker. Since all the boards have the same numbers on them, all of the children will finish at the same time.

**Concentration:** Place the cards face down and have the children find the pairs. Children can play this game with either the dot cards or the numeral cards.

**Match-Ups:** Match the dot cards to the bingo boards or the numeral cards to the dot cards.

## What They Learn

Cognitive development skills: Most children begin to count between ages two and three. At first the counting is rote, that is, it is a memorized routine, such as "Onetwothreefourfivesix!" By age three or four, a child's counting has become more precise. By now he most likely has a basic understanding of one-to-one correspondence between a short sequence of number words and the items they represent. This indicates he is on the verge of mastering correct counting.

## Extending the Learning

This game has many variations, and your knowledge of a child's mathematical abilities will help you decide which one is most appropriate for his level of development. To enhance a preschooler's counting skills, for example, play the game with counters. Give him a pile of buttons, pennies, or poker chips, and ask him to place the appropriate number of counters on either side of the bingo cards.

## What You Need

☐ three pieces of tagboard (12 by 18 inches each)

☐ ruler

☐ marker

☐ black coding dots

- ☐ scissors
- ☐ clear contact paper
- ☐ pencil
- ☐ bingo markers (such as pennies, buttons, or poker chips)
- ☐ box to hold the cards, numerals, and markers

## How to Make It

1. Using a ruler, mark off twenty-four 3-inch squares on each of the three pieces of tagboard.

2. On one of the large pieces of tagboard, make four sets of dots that represent numbers 1 through 6. Cover with clear contact paper.

3. On the second piece of tagboard, print four sets of the numerals 1 through 6 in twenty-four squares. Cover with clear contact paper and cut into 3-by-3-inch playing cards.

4. To make the bingo cards, cut the third piece of tagboard into four 9-by-6-inch pieces.

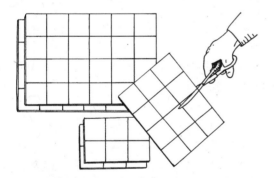

5. Mark off six squares on each side of the card. On the first side, place one to six dots in the squares, varying the placement on the cards but keeping patterns for each number the

same as on the large card. On the reverse side of the bingo cards, write the numerals 1 to 6 in the squares. Cover the large pieces of tagboard and the bingo cards with clear contact paper.

## Variations

To use with plastic numerals: Match the plastic numerals to either the dot side or the numeral side of the bingo cards. Plastic numerals can be placed in a row and all the playing cards that match that numeral can be placed in that row also.

To use with counters: Add counting items such as buttons, pennies, or poker chips, and place the appropriate number of counters on either side of the bingo cards.

To use with playing cards: Place a label or sticker of the suits (club, heart, diamond, and spade) on each bingo card. Divide a deck of cards and place the cards from aces through sixes face down on the table. Children draw a card from the pile and find its place on the bingo card, matching the suit and number.

# Bottle-Cap Counters

## Who

Preschoolers

## About the Toy

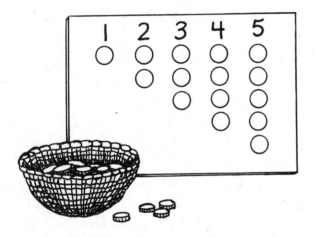

These bottle-cap counters can be used in a variety of counting and matching games. For a number-matching game, have the children arrange the bottle caps in rows, counting out the appropriate number. Make a color-matching game by writing each numeral in a different color. Children then use bottle caps that match the indicated color.

## What They Learn

Cognitive development skills: In learning to count, a preschooler may experiment with different strategies, such as counting on her fingers. Later, when learning addition and subtraction, she may continue to use her fingers to help her add or subtract. But as she learns other more efficient methods, ones that result in quicker, more accurate solutions, she will give up using her fingers and will rely on her memory to help her find the answers.

## Extending the Learning

This game helps children learn about numbers by actually counting out the correct quantity for each numeral. For younger preschoolers, use numbers 1 to 5; for older preschoolers, add 6 to 10. You will learn a lot about each child's skills in mathematical thinking as you observe the children playing this game together.

## What You Need

☐ tagboard
☐ markers
☐ fifteen plastic bottle caps
☐ basket

## How to Make It

1. Write the numerals 1 to 5 across the top of the tagboard. Under each numeral, use a bottle cap to trace the appropriate number of circles. (For color matching games, use colored markers to write numerals and trace circles.)

2. Store the bottle caps in a small basket.

## Variation

Sort the bottle caps by colors into matching bowls. Write the numerals 1 to 5 on pieces of paper. Fold up the pieces and place them in a bowl. Have the children draw a number and arrange that number of bottle caps on the board or on the table next to the number. Add larger numbers (6 to 10 and higher) for older children. Encourage children to make up their own games.

Make sure plastic bottles are disposed of with your other recycling.

# Counting Circles

## Who

Preschoolers

## About the Toy

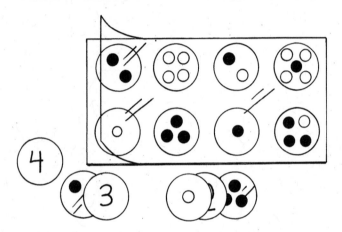

This activity gives children—either individually or in a small group—practice in comparing and matching sets of dots by number or color. It also helps children associate specific numerals with the corresponding quantity. In a small group game, place the master playing board in the center and deal the playing cards around the group. Point to a circle on the playing board and describe it by color and number (for example, green fours). All of the children with those cards place them on the matching master playing-board space. Play other games using a single category (for example, all red or all twos). The children with cards matching the category place them on the board.

Use this activity to match sets. Match the coding dots to corresponding sets of coding dots or to the appropriate numeral written on the other side of the playing cards.

## What They Learn

Language and communication development skills: When children play mathematical games, they develop not only their mathematical skills but also their mathematical vocabularies. For example, in describing addition problems, they will begin to use terms such as *add, total,* and *altogether,* and in describing subtraction problems, they will use the terms *take away* and *subtract.* In fact, any activity involving other children or adults will enhance a preschooler's vocabulary. Even simple conversations with others will introduce him to new words and ideas and will challenge him to practice his ever-expanding language and communication skills.

## Extending the Learning

When you play mathematical games with a child, use it as an opportunity to further develop his vocabulary. Ask him questions about the sets of circles used in this game using the terms *more than, less than,* and *the same,* for example, "Does this green set have more circles than this red set?" and "What about these two sets? How many are in each set? Three? Yes, they are the same. You're right."

## What You Need

☐ two pieces of tagboard (8 by 16 inches each)

☐ ½-inch coding dots in a variety of colors

☐ marker

☐ scissors

☐ 3-inch-diameter circle pattern

☐ clear contact paper

## How to Make It

### PLAYING BOARD

1. Trace two rows of 3-inch-diameter circles on one piece of tagboard.

2. Place coding dots in the circles. Use different colors for each circle, but keep the dot arrangements consistent for each number. Cover the entire playing board with clear contact paper.

### PLAYING CARDS

1. On the other piece of tagboard, trace two rows of 3-inch-diameter circles. (You may make as many pieces as you wish, because more than one circle can match the circle on the playing board.)

2. Place coding dots in the circles to match the circles on the playing board (both in colors and number of dots used). Cover cards with clear contact paper and cut out each circle.

3. On the back of each circle, write the numeral that corresponds to the number of dots. (For younger children, write the numeral in the same color as the dots. For older children, write the numerals in black.) Cover the backs with clear contact paper.

## Variation

For a large group or for older children, make additional playing boards and increase number variations (using numbers 1 to 8). Make additional playing cards as well. Older children could use this as a bingo game.

When you buy stickers and other consumable items, try to buy them in bulk. Buying in bulk saves on packaging that usually ends up in landfills.

GREEN IDEA · GREEN IDEA

# Visiting-the-Zoo Board Game

## Who

Preschoolers

## About the Toy

This game provides an opportunity for children to practice counting as they move their game pieces along the path. It also provides opportunities to discuss the animals, what they do, and the experiences that will be part of the trip. And they get to imitate animal sounds! This not only helps to better prepare the children for the experience, but also greatly increases language learning by promoting verbal expression and creativity.

Two to four children can play this game. To introduce it and promote discussion of the topic, you should first play the game with the children.

Place the board and cards in the center of the group. Each player takes turns picking a card and moving their game piece the corresponding number of spaces along the path. If a player lands on an animal picture, the group names and discusses that

animal and everyone imitates the sound it makes (for example, a lion's roar). When a child draws a card with a snack picture on it, that player's game piece stays put and the player pretends to eat the pictured snack. The game continues until everyone finishes visiting the zoo and lands on the going home space.

Use this game in preparation for a trip to the zoo or a similar outing (for example, a farm with animals, or a mall with barnyard animals). You can also use this game for review after the trip.

Very young children may not be interested in the rules of the game but will enjoy moving their game pieces along the path, making the animal sounds, and making up stories about the animals, all of which may help hold their attention.

## What They Learn

Social and emotional development skills: Preschool-age children are still learning how to get along with their peers—what it means to help them, share with them, and cooperate with them. Games with rules can present a challenge to children of this age, since their inclination is to disregard the rules and invent their own. In addition, concepts such as following directions, taking turns, and completing tasks may be new to some children.

## Extending the Learning

Your awareness of the developmental realities of preschoolers will enable you to choose games and activities that are appropriate and that enhance their learning. Since you know, for example, that games with rules can be challenging for three- and four-year-olds, consider offering them rule-bound activities that are more casual and intrinsically motivating. Games such as Duck, Duck, Goose and Musical Chairs, which involve physical movement but still function under a loose set of rules, would be good introductions to games with rules and also entertaining for children of this age.

## What You Need

- ☐ large piece of tagboard
- ☐ felt-tip markers
- ☐ pictures or stickers of zoo animals
- ☐ clear contact paper
- ☐ twelve index cards (3 by 5 inches each)
- ☐ scissors
- ☐ glue
- ☐ small coding dots
- ☐ magazine pictures of snacks
- ☐ game pieces

## How to Make It

### PLAYING BOARD

1. Draw a curving path on the tagboard from one corner to the opposite corner. Divide the path into 1-inch squares. At the start, draw an arrow and print the word *Zoo*. At the finish, draw a picture of a bus or car and write *Going Home*.

2. In every sixth or eighth space along the path, place a picture of a different animal.

3. To make it look like a zoo, decorate the playing board with other animal pictures. Cover the game board with clear contact paper.

4. For game pieces, use such items as beans, bingo pieces, buttons, flat beads, bottle caps, corks, rocks, spools, thimbles, large washers, or pieces from other games.

### PLAYING CARDS

1. Cut each index card in half. On sixteen to eighteen of the cards, write a number from 1 to 3. Put the same number of coding dots on each card. Cut out the pictures of snacks and glue them to the remaining six to eight blank cards. Consider using magazine pictures of such snacks as ice cream bars, pretzels, apples, and popcorn.

2. Cover the cards with clear contact paper.

## Variations

To vary the game, make the paths square, circular, diagonal, snail shaped, or any combination of these. Increase the difficulty of the game by using cutoffs or arrows that direct players to longer paths.

To change the tasks, have children match shapes, colors, numbers, rhymes (depicted visually), textures, patterns, letters, or letter sounds to pictures.

To change the format, have the children use dice or a spinner with colors coded to the game board, or have them pull numbers from a sock or box.

Board game themes are unlimited. You can make a game board to introduce or explain any topic from how plants become products in our grocery stores to the route a letter takes from your home to a friend's. Some other examples:

**Trips:** Going to the hospital, fire station, apple orchard, airport, or library.

**Books:** *Magic Tree House* or *The Magic School Bus* series.

**Products:** How milk, corn, or potatoes go from a farm to our table. How chairs are made from trees. How peanut butter is made at the peanut butter plant.

Consider making the playing board from old file folders, old place mats, or old game boards and cover them with contact paper.

# Top the Box

## Who

Preschoolers

## About the Toy

This game helps children recognize numerals and the quantity each numeral represents. Putting boxes together provides practice using small-motor skills, and recognizing and matching sizes provides practice using perception skills. The game provides an opportunity to discuss and illustrate many concepts such as shape, fit, open, close, inside, top, bottom, empty, full, and how many.

This is an independent activity in which one or two children try to find the number sets that go together. Spread out the boxes in random fashion so the tops and bottoms are visible. (The boxes should be different enough in dimension so that each top fits only one bottom, making the game self-correcting.) After matching the correct bottoms and tops, children may put the indicated number of beads or other items in each box.

## What They Learn

Language and communication development skills: Children's play is the vehicle through which they learn and develop, and this is particularly true when it comes to language development. Play motivates children to use and practice language, and it encourages verbal thinking. When children play, they experiment with how language is used, and they try out new words and concepts.

## Extending the Learning

Group play is an especially rich language-learning environment for children. Through their social interactions, children share with others about themselves and their experiences with the world as well as develop an appreciation for others and how their experiences are the same or different. Your involvement can enhance their language development, but be careful not to step in and take charge. Watching from the sidelines and occasionally asking children open-ended questions about what they are doing is a great way to enhance language learning.

## What You Need

☐ small boxes with lids, of similar size and shape but different enough so each top fits only one mate (jewelry boxes work well)

☐ small objects to place inside the box (such as beads, pegs, or buttons)

☐ markers

☐ small coding dots or gummed stars

☐ scissors

## How to Make It

1. Inside the bottom of each box, write a numeral from 1 to 6.

2. Write the same numeral on the inside of the box's lid. For older preschoolers, you can omit writing the numerals on the inside of the box's lid.

3. Place the corresponding number of dots or stars on the top of the box's lid.

## Variation

Mount matching pieces of colored construction paper inside each box and its lid. Let the children match the colors, or they can use the boxes to sort small objects by color.

Fresh fruit offers children, and adults, higher nutritional value and uses less packaging than fruit juice blends, which are often made with high-fructose corn syrup. Consider serving fresh fruits that are in season—chances are they have not traveled very far, which saves energy too!

GREEN IDEA · GREEN IDEA ·

# Painter's Palette

## Who

Preschoolers

## About the Toy

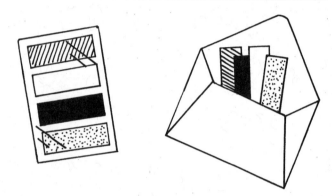

This activity provides practice in matching colors and learning to recognize differences in colors. Have the children spread out the boards and find the pieces that match each color. You can also make up games using color samples in various shades of all colors. For example, you might have children look for the lightest and darkest shade of blue or find the red that matches the crayon.

## What They Learn

Sensory perception development skills: Learning to recognize different colors and their names is one of preschoolers' developmental tasks. In this activity, children's visual-perception skills are enhanced as they practice matching colors and recognizing the different shades and tints of the same color.

## Extending the Learning

Adjusting this color-recognition activity to a child's developmental level will ensure greater success. For a younger preschooler, make sure the colors on the boards are very different. As her skills increase, make and use boards that require more precise color discrimination, such as recognizing different shades of the same color. For an older preschooler, set out large boxes of crayons or colored pencils and paper, and see whether she can create shades that match the colors on the boards.

## What You Need

☐ paint color sample cards, two of each color

☐ unlined index cards (5 by 8 inches each)

☐ glue

☐ clear contact paper

☐ scissors

☐ business-size envelopes

☐ crayons

## How to Make It

1. Cut apart the paint color samples. Be sure to have two of each.

2. Select the colors you want to use (either different or similar). Glue one set of colors onto an index card. Leave the other set of colors in pieces. Make several sets.

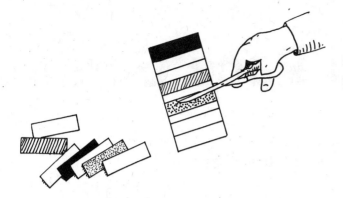

3. Cover the index cards and the individual pieces with clear contact paper.

4. Store the index cards and the individual pieces in envelopes according to their colors.

## Variation

Make palettes that show the shades of various colors. At the top of a 9-by-12-inch sheet of paper, paint a stripe of one color. Dip the paintbrush in water, wipe the brush against the side of the water dish to remove the excess, and then paint another stripe. The second stripe will be one shade lighter than the first. Keep repeating this process until the sheet is covered with stripes—each one a lighter shade of the same color—until all color is removed. Make similar palettes for many colors and let the children discover which colors last longer and which ones lose their color faster.

Ask your local paint supply store for permission to set up a used color-card collection box. People often take these cards and return later to buy their chosen colors. If they know they can recycle the cards, they may be inclined to bring them back and drop them in the box. Once a month or so, you can pick up the color cards in the box and use them with the children.

GREEN IDEA • GREEN IDEA

# Stop-and-Go Race Game

## Who

Preschoolers

## About the Toy

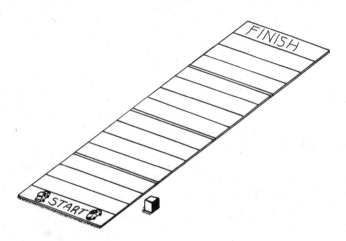

This game helps teach children to associate the colors red and green with stop and go. Use it when you are teaching about traffic lights or as part of an interest center about cars, traffic, or transportation. Children love to play with small cars, and this game encourages them to use cars cooperatively in a simple game that models new ways to use cars in play.

Playing simple, noncompetitive games gives children practice in taking turns and following the rules—concepts that preschoolers are just beginning to explore and do not fully understand.

Children play this game two at a time. Each child chooses a small car to use as a playing piece and places it on the start line. The first player tosses a cube that has red and green sides. If the color is green, that player's car moves ahead one space. If red shows, the player's car does not move. The game ends when both cars have crossed the finish line.

## What They Learn

Social and emotional development skills: When a child is able to understand the viewpoints and feelings of others, his ability to get along with others improves. Since some preschoolers are still acquiring this ability, simple, noncompetitive games are often the best way for them to practice taking turns, following rules, and behaving in a manner that is beneficial to the group—all examples of prosocial behaviors they will learn in time.

## Extending the Learning

Ongoing social situations are good opportunities for talking with preschoolers about perspective-taking, such as welcoming a new child to the group. For example, you might say, "James, this is Ali. She is new and doesn't know anybody yet. How do you think she feels? What might make her feel better?" Another approach is to ask a child how her actions might make another child feel: "Mei, you grabbed the car Jess was waiting to use. How do you suppose Jess feels right now?"

## What You Need

☐ four sheets of tagboard (8 by 11 inches each) or four file folders

☐ cloth tape

☐ marker

☐ ruler

☐ clear contact paper

☐ small wooden cube

☐ paintbrush

- ☐ scissors
- ☐ red and green paint
- ☐ two small cars

## How to Make It

### GAME BOARD

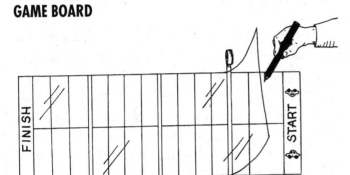

1. Join the tagboard pieces to one another with cloth tape to form one 8-by-44-inch piece. For strength and durability, be sure to tape both the front and back sides of the seams. Cloth tape allows the board to fold easily for storage.

2. Using the ruler, mark off a section at each end. At one end, print the word *start* and draw two cars. At the other end, print the word *finish*.

3. Draw a dividing line down the middle of the board to form two lanes. Mark off intervals across the board (be sure the cars fit into the intervals). Cover the racetrack with the contact paper.

### STOP-AND-GO CUBE

1. Paint two sides of the cube red and four sides green. You can use any small wooden cube, or you can make your own cube from milk cartons (see p. 204).

Make the game board out of an old sheet. Use fabric markers or tape to mark off the spaces for the racetrack.

GREEN IDEA • GREEN IDEA

# Cracker Game

## Who

Preschoolers

## About the Toy

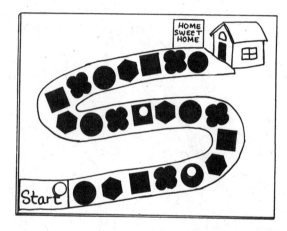

This game helps develop awareness of shapes in common objects and encourages children to recognize likenesses and differences in shapes. It provides practice at turn taking; playing a simple, non-competitive game; and following directions.

Use this game board with both small and large groups of children for a variety of games. For a small-group game, place a stack of the playing cards face down. Have children take turns drawing cards and moving their playing piece to the next shape along the path that matches the card drawn. They can return cards to the bottom of the pile after each turn. Each child in turn continues along the path until all players reach home place.

The Extending the Learning activity (described in the next column) promotes social interaction and may stimulate discussion about food-related shapes.

## What They Learn

Cognitive development skills: One of the mathematical skills children develop during the preschool years is the ability to recognize and name 2-D and 3-D shapes. They can talk about some of the characteristics of shapes and recognize their similarities and differences. Shape-matching activities like this one encourage the development of geometry-related skills.

## Extending the Learning

Helping children recognize that math is everywhere is a great way to reinforce their mathematics learning. For example, play this game at snacktime by arranging crackers of different shapes directly on a sanitized board and having the children take turns drawing a card and eating a matching cracker from the game board. Ask the children about some of the shapes on the table around them: "What shape is this napkin?" "What is the shape on the bottom of our cups called?" "What shape is this table?"

## What You Need

- ☐ tagboard for game board, cards, and patterns (one piece 12 by 18 inches and one 9 by 12 inches)
- ☐ marker
- ☐ small objects for playing pieces (such as buttons or beads)
- ☐ a variety of different-shaped crackers
- ☐ clear contact paper

□ scissors or paper cutter

□ ruler

## How to Make It

1. On the large piece of tagboard, draw the game board as illustrated.

2. On the other piece of tagboard, trace each cracker shape and cut out the shapes to use as patterns.

3. Use the patterns to trace a sequence of shapes along the path on the game board. Spread them out so you have twenty to twenty-four outlines on the path. Cover the board with clear contact paper.

4. For the playing cards, measure two ½-inch squares on the tagboard. Using the patterns, trace a shape in each square. Make at least four playing cards of each shape. Cover the cards with clear contact paper. Cut out the cards.

Buy or make a simple compost bin with chicken wire. Instead of throwing away crackers that children take but don't eat, supply a dump bucket that children can put crackers and other uneaten snack foods in. Then empty the bucket into the compost bin.

GREEN IDEA • GREEN IDEA •

# Magnet Mysteries

## Who

Preschoolers

## About the Toy

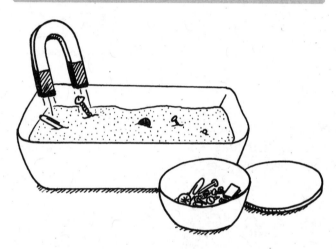

This activity provides a fun way for children to learn about and experiment with magnets. After an initial demonstration, children bury or hide metal objects in the sand and then use magnets to get them out. The metal objects must be either iron, steel, or copper for the magnet to work. The magnets should not have to touch the sand but should be strong enough to pull out the objects. Strong bar, horseshoe, or "cow" magnets work well. Children can count the items they put into the sand to see if they have retrieved all of them. To catch loose sand, place all of the items used in this activity on a tray or cookie sheet.

If more than one child is participating, have children bury objects in a sandbox and give several children magnets to see how many items they can retrieve.

For a variation, include some items the magnet will not pick up. Talk about what happened and why the magnet didn't work on those items.

## What They Learn

Approaches to learning development skills: Young children's problem solving is often compared with the problem solving of scientists, since both seek answers to questions that may seem trivial and unanswerable to others. Children's questions might include "Do fish drink water?" and "Why is the sky blue?" When children experiment, observe, question, and discuss results, they are demonstrating the basics of scientific inquiry.

## Extending the Learning

Because magnets are particularly fascinating toys for children, they make ideal learning tools. As children hide and recover the metal and nonmetal objects in the sand, they are experimenting with cause and effect. They are also using fine-motor skills as they search for items in an environment that provides sensory stimulation. Counting and remembering whether all of the objects have been found enhances preschoolers' cognitive and memory skills too.

## What You Need

☐ large plastic container with lid

☐ tray or cookie sheet

☐ clean sand

- [ ] small metal objects (nails, screws, paper clips, or ball bearings)
- [ ] nonmetal objects (such as plastic and aluminum toys)
- [ ] small tub with lid
- [ ] strong magnets

## How to Make It

1. Clean out the large container and let it dry.

2. Fill the container half to two-thirds full with sand and place it on a tray.

3. Collect metal and nonmetal objects and magnets. These items can be placed in clean tubs for storage.

Use clean margarine tubs for storage containers. Use a permanent marker to label the sides and top and stack them together in a storage closet.

GREEN IDEA · GREEN IDEA ·

# Dots to Dinosaurs

## Who

Preschoolers

## About the Toy

This activity teaches auditory discrimination skills by providing practice in matching sounds for the letter *d*. Sequencing by size encourages visual discrimination and problem-solving skills.

In this activity, children match a sequence of dinosaur images to a similar sequence of dots. First have children find all the small dinosaurs and put them next to the small dot, then have them continue to the medium and large dots. Be sure to say the words *dots* and *dinosaurs*. Add other small, medium, and large pictures of things that begin with the *d* sound, such as dolls, ducks, dresses, and dogs.

## What They Learn

Language and communication development skills: Phonics refers to the relationship between letters of the alphabet (symbols) and the sounds they represent. Evidence suggests that exposure to age-appropriate phonics-related activities at an early age can facilitate children's reading and spelling development.

## Extending the Learning

For children to develop positive dispositions toward reading, prereading experiences such as letter/sound recognition must actively engage them in the learning process. The younger the child, the more important it is to employ a variety of teaching methods and activities. Dots to Dinosaurs is one activity you can use to enhance a preschooler's auditory discrimination skills. If the child easily grasps the concept of the letter *d* and its sound, consider making additional picture cards of other letters of the alphabet.

## What You Need

- ☐ file folder
- ☐ marker
- ☐ small, medium, and large pictures of dinosaurs
- ☐ scissors
- ☐ glue
- ☐ tagboard
- ☐ clear contact paper
- ☐ manila envelope
- ☐ paper clip

## How to Make It

1. Write the letter *d* on the front cover of the file folder. Draw three dots along the left edge of the open file folder: one small, one medium,

and one large. Leave ample space between dots. Cover with contact paper.

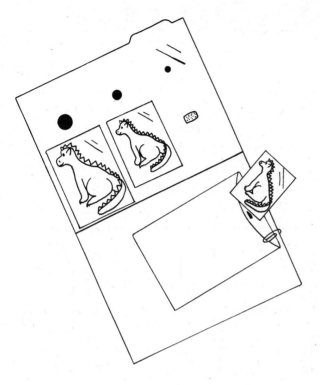

2. Cut out three dinosaur pictures: one small, one medium, and one large. (Wrapping paper, books, catalogs, or stickers are good sources for dinosaur pictures.) Glue the pictures to a piece of tagboard, cover them with clear contact paper, and cut them out.

3. If desired, attach a Velcro strip underneath each dot on the file folder. Mount small pieces of Velcro on the back of each picture. Store the pictures in a manila envelope and attach it to the file folder with a paper clip.

## Variation

Make additional picture cards to match with items beginning with the letter *d* and other letters. For example, for the letter *s*, draw stars (instead of dots) on the file folder, and match them to pictures of shells. For the letter *b*, use balls and bears.

Consider planting native grasses and flowers. You won't attract dinosaurs, but native flowers are often welcomed sources of food for butterflies, birds, and insects.

GREEN IDEA • GREEN IDEA •

# Picture Partners

## Who

Preschoolers

## About the Toy

This activity helps children recognize likenesses and differences in pictures. It encourages the development of observation and memory skills, increases concentration, and introduces the concept of a set of items—a premath skill. You can make games relating to a particular theme, which helps build vocabularies and illustrates the variety of specific items in the broader category. For example, when playing a game using pictures of trucks, discuss features of cement trucks, dump trucks, moving vans, tow trucks, and pickup trucks.

Note that the matches are harder to find if all the pair sets illustrate the varieties within a single category, such as flowers (a pair of roses, a pair of chrysanthemums, a pair of tulips). Conversely, matches are easier if the pair sets are obviously different (for example, a pair of flowers, a pair of animals, a pair of trucks).

To use as a concentration game for two or three children, place the cards face down on a level surface.

Each child takes a turn flipping over two cards so everyone can see the pictures on them. If the pictures match, the child collects the pair and takes another turn. If they don't match, the child turns the cards face down in the same spot and the play moves to the next child. Repeat until the children have paired and collected all cards. (Initially, you'll probably need to play the game in order to introduce it and the turn-taking process and to encourage the children to remember where cards are.)

A simple game for younger children is to spread out the cards face up and let each child collect one pair for each turn. You also can use the cards as an individual activity in which a child arranges all the cards in pairs.

## What They Learn

Cognitive development skills: With the increase in children's ability to focus comes the increase in their ability to remember things. Short-term memory increases significantly during early childhood. Several characteristics determine the effectiveness of a child's memory, including age, attitude, health, motivation, and previous knowledge.

## Extending the Learning

Forgetting there was once a time when our memory skills were not as finely tuned as they are now, memory is something we all take for granted. Three- and four-year-old children are still in the process of acquiring the more sophisticated memory skills of adults, and memory games such as Picture Partners help foster their concentration and memory skills.

## What You Need

- ☐ tagboard
- ☐ twelve pairs of matching stickers
- ☐ scissors
- ☐ ruler
- ☐ pencil
- ☐ clear contact paper

## How to Make It

1. Rule off and draw twenty-four 1½-inch squares on the tagboard.

2. Mount stickers in the center of each square on the tagboard. Be sure to use two of each sticker.

3. Cover the tagboard sheet with clear contact paper and cut out the squares to create twelve pairs of matching cards.

## Variation

To make an easier game that produces more matching pairs, make six sets of four matching cards instead of twelve matching pairs. Children still try to find matching pairs, but since there are four matching cards in each set, they get more matches.

Instead of using stickers, draw simple illustrations showing familiar items or cut shapes from scraps of construction paper.

GREEN IDEA • GREEN IDEA

# Preschoolers
# and Schoolagers

# Airplane

## Who

Preschoolers and schoolagers

## About the Toy

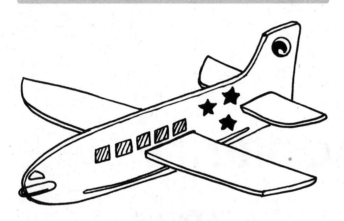

Constructing these planes can help children learn basic principles of flight. Show the children pictures of new and old airplanes and discuss what they look like and how their designs have changed. Encourage the children to name the parts of the planes.

Set out Styrofoam trays, an airplane pattern, and ballpoint pens. Encourage the children to press hard as they trace the pattern into the Styrofoam. Vary the size, number, and placement of wings to see how these differences affect flight. To avoid ripping the Styrofoam, help the children make the slits for the wings and insert them. Older preschoolers and schoolagers can make these airplanes and take them outside to fly.

## What They Learn

Approaches to learning development skills: Flight is a fascinating concept for many young children.

Most preschoolers and schoolagers are developed enough in their thinking skills to be able to fully participate in this activity involving the principles of flight. For example, they can be encouraged to think about and experiment with how the size, shape, number of parts, and placement of parts affect a Styrofoam airplane's ability to fly. In the block area, the toy planes can become part of a dramatic play scenario involving airports and air transportation.

## Extending the Learning

This activity can evolve into something quite different for each child, depending on the child's developmental level and interests. For example, one child might discover through trial and error that there are basic design flaws in the original airplane pattern. She may end up designing her own pattern using slightly different materials. Another child might enjoy using her fine-motor skills to cut out, assemble, and decorate her plane. Children are more motivated to learn about things that interest them and things they enjoy, so be sure to follow their lead as they work to create and play with these toy airplanes.

## What You Need

☐ tagboard

☐ Styrofoam trays

☐ ballpoint pen

☐ scissors

☐ paper clips

☐ clear contact paper (optional)

☐ markers and stickers (optional)

## How to Make It

1. Draw several copies of airplane parts onto tagboard. Cut out the patterns. (Help the children as needed.)

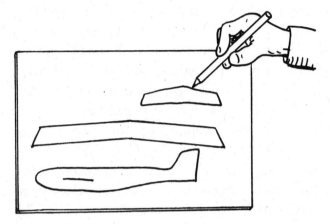

2. Place the patterns on the trays and trace them with a ballpoint pen. Cut out the plane pieces.

3. For longer lasting planes, lay the plane pieces on the sticky side of clear contact paper. Lay another piece of clear contact paper on top. Press together, making sure the sticky parts of the contact paper are tightly joined all around each piece. Cut the pieces out, leaving ⅛ to ¼ inch of contact paper around each piece.

4. Draw two lines in the body of the plane where the wings should be inserted. Using the point of a pair of scissors, cut slits along the lines. Carefully insert the wings.

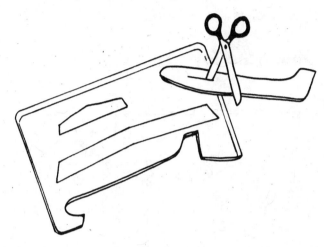

5. Put the paper clip on the nose of the plane. Decorate the plane with stickers, decals, or markers.

If a Styrofoam airplane breaks in two, tape it together and keep using it. If it breaks beyond repair, reuse the pieces in packaging, or, if possible, recycle them.

GREEN IDEA · GREEN IDEA ·

# Dot-to-Dot

## Who

Preschoolers and schoolagers

## About the Toy

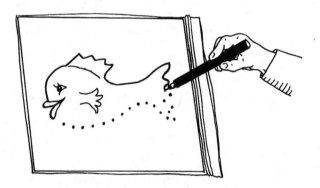

This activity provides a method to prolong the life of dot-to-dot or tracing pages from coloring books so children can use them more than once. Select a variety of tracing or dot-to-dot pictures and show the children how to insert one picture into a resealable plastic bag. Children trace the picture or complete the dot-to-dot using washable markers or erasable crayons. When completed, a child can use a damp sponge or washcloth to wipe off the plastic bag and trace the picture again or turn it over and trace the other side. As they work, encourage the children to guess what the pictures in the dot-to-dots might be.

## What They Learn

Physical and motor development skills: The development of fine-motor skills during the preschool and schoolage years allows children to create drawings that contain more details and that more closely resemble the real world. Rhoda Kellogg is an early childhood educator who has observed and guided young children's artistic efforts for decades. According to Kellogg, there are four stages of artistic development in young children, all of which are meaningful, orderly, and structured. Four- and five-year-old children typically fall within the final stage of artistic development—the pictorial stage. It is during the pictorial stage that children's drawings begin to contain objects, animals, and people that others can recognize. (Kellogg, R. *Understanding Children's Art: Readings in Developmental Psychology Today*. Del Mar, CA: CRM, 1970.)

## Extending the Learning

Tracing activities, such as this one, encourage the development of children's small-muscle skills as well as hand-eye coordination. After children become comfortable connecting the dots to form pictures, you can enhance the activity by having children create their own dot-to-dot pictures. Children may also enjoy sharing their dot-to-dot creations with one another and watching the mystery pictures take shape.

## What You Need

- ☐ numbered dot-to-dot or tracing pages from coloring books
- ☐ resealable plastic bags
- ☐ tagboard
- ☐ wipe-off or washable markers or erasable crayons
- ☐ scissors
- ☐ glue
- ☐ sponges or washcloths

## How to Make It

1. Cut out several dot-to-dot or tracing pages from coloring books. (Use pictures of varying difficulty to match the children's abilities.) If the pictures are on only one side of the page, glue one page to each side of a sheet of tagboard. If there is a picture on both sides of the page, proceed to step 2.

2. Place each dot-to-dot sheet in a resealable bag.

3. Arrange bags, markers, and sponges on a table for the children to select and use.

## Variation

Make pattern cards using the children's names. Insert these cards into bags and let the children practice tracing their names.

Dispose of magazines and coloring books with your other recycling.

# Copycat Covers

## Who

Preschoolers and schoolagers

## About the Toy

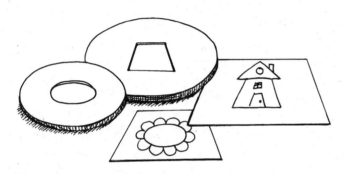

Tracing encourages the development of hand-eye coordination and small-motor skills. This activity helps children learn shapes or pattern discrimination and provides a starting point for them to use shapes or symbols in their own creations. These patterns allow children who want to create a precise shape without adult assistance feel successful.

Invite the children to use patterns to trace shapes on paper. They can use the patterns singly or in combination to create designs. Children can color or decorate the shapes or designs in any way they wish. Children can also use the patterns for spatter, roller, or sponge painting.

## What They Learn

Cognitive development skills: Tracing a variety of shapes on paper reinforces early mathematical concepts such as shape recognition and classifying, both of which are developmentally appropriate tasks for children this age. Children are also enhancing memory skills as they create designs and other things from the various shapes on their papers.

## Extending the Learning

You can enhance children's learning by asking them to identify shapes in the environment that are similar to the ones they are tracing on their papers. For example, say to a child, "You told me the shape you are tracing is a circle, and you're right; it is a circle. Show me something in this room that is shaped like a circle. Yes, the big clock on the wall is a circle too. Let's look around for other things that are shaped like circles."

## What You Need

☐ plastic lids (such as those from ice cream containers or coffee cans)

☐ permanent marker

☐ scissors or X-Acto knife (if made by adult)

☐ cutting board or cardboard

☐ paper

☐ markers and crayons

## How to Make It

1. Draw shapes with the permanent marker on the plastic lids.

2. Place the lid on a cutting surface. Use an X-Acto knife or scissors to cut out the shapes.

3. Give children paper, markers, and crayons to make pictures using the lids.

## Variation

Take the shapes outside and invite the children to use them with chalk on the sidewalk.

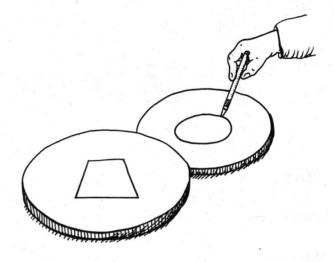

Turn broken crayon pieces into rainbow crayons by removing the paper (and recycling it!) and melting the crayons in a glass custard cup in the microwave or in an old muffin tin at a low temperature in the oven.

GREEN IDEA · GREEN IDEA ·

# Money Matters

## Who

Preschoolers and schoolagers

## About the Toy

Children can use this activity to count and match amounts of play money or paper circles ("pennies") to the amount each coin represents (for example, five pennies equal one nickel). Children can make rubbings of coins and then turn them into play money.

Use the cards to see if children recognize the value of specific coins. Hold up the cards with the numeral covered (fold the lower card over the upper one) and see if the children can recognize the coin and tell how many cents (or pennies) it is worth. Use extra sets of the money cards to demonstrate the combinations that make up the value of the larger coins.

## What They Learn

Cognitive development and language and communication development skills: Most four- and five-year-olds have had experiences involving money,

but they cannot always identify the amounts represented by the different coins. Hands-on activities such as this one, during which children hold coins and count out how much each coin is worth, help them develop a more concrete understanding of the values of each of the coins. Children also expand their vocabularies by learning the names of coins and hearing words associated with money computations, such as *equal to* and *altogether*.

## Extending the Learning

When children are using play money, such as in make-believe activities involving stores and banks, listen for how they identify and use the play money. How do they dispense money or count out change? If you are playing with them, use it as an opportunity to reinforce their learning. Say to a child, for example, "You've given me ten pennies. I'd rather not carry around so many coins. Please find me other coins in the cash register that are equal to ten pennies."

## What You Need

☐ tagboard (four pieces 6½ by 7 inches each and four pieces 4½ by 5 inches each)

☐ forty-two pennies, one quarter, one dime, one nickel

☐ glue

☐ marker

☐ scissors

☐ clear contact paper

☐ paper

☐ crayon

☐ small box or sturdy envelope

☐ tape

## How to Make It

1. Glue the nickel to the top of one of the larger pieces of tagboard. Print the word *nickel* under it and the number 5 at the bottom. Glue the dime, a penny, and the quarter to the top of the other three pieces of tagboard. Include the corresponding word and number under the coin. Cover the pieces of tagboard with clear contact paper.

2. On the smaller boards, represent the value of the larger coin by gluing on the equivalent number of pennies (one for the penny, five for the nickel, ten for the dime, and twenty-five for the quarter). Cover the boards with clear contact paper.

3. Tape the small card with the pennies to the large card. When you fold up the lower card, the pennies will not show and should cover the number.

4. Use coin rubbings to create play money. Place pennies under sheets of paper and rub over the coins with the side of a crayon. Cut out the rubbings. Store in a small box or sturdy envelope.

## Variation

Show the different combinations of coins that equal the value of a single coin. Make five cards with five pennies on them and a few with nickels and dimes. For example, the dime card could show two nickels or one nickel and five pennies. The quarter card could show five nickels or two dimes and one nickel.

Save money and help keep plastics out of landfills by bringing your lunch in a reusable container.

# Tic-Tac-Toe

## Who

Preschoolers and schoolagers

## About the Toy

This activity helps develop many premath and logical thinking skills, including sequencing, sorting same and different, and counting. It also illustrates the concept of a set, because three of the same item (X or O) in a specific order are required to score. Older children may use the activity to develop planning strategies.

The format of this activity makes it possible for more children to play. It also makes it easier to keep track of completed rows and introduces a record-keeping system.

Two to four children, ages four and older, can play this game. If four children are playing, have an X team and an O team. Divide the X and O cards into separate piles. Children take turns placing Xs or Os on the board, trying to get three of a kind in as many rows as they can. On a score pad, keep track of how many rows of three Xs and three Os there are. Count rows in all directions—vertical, horizontal, and diagonal. If there are no rows of

three Xs or Os, give a point to an animal (for example, a cat) drawn at the top of a third column.

Preschoolers will not try to prevent one another from making complete rows. Schoolagers will develop strategies and be more concerned about winning.

## What They Learn

Approaches to learning development skills: The play of children between the ages of four and five is just beginning to involve rules, and most children are still in the process of developing an understanding of rules. Some may even become quite rigid when enforcing rules, which can disrupt play and become a source of conflict. This is because they are not yet able to apply rules in a flexible, reasonable way.

## Extending the Learning

Group games teach children about cooperation, getting along with others, and working together toward a common goal. Since you know that children this age may have difficulty playing group games with rules, be sure to observe their play often. Look for opportunities to help them understand some of the social guidelines that are an inherent part of games with rules by modeling how to understand and apply rules in ways that promote cooperation, learning, and fun.

## What You Need

☐ several pieces of tagboard (each 9 inches square)

☐ ruler

☐ markers

☐ scissors

☐ clear contact paper

☐ score pad and pencil

## How to Make It

1. On the tagboard, draw nine 1-inch squares. Make two boards for team play.

2. Divide two more pieces of tagboard into nine 1-inch squares. On one piece, draw Xs in each square. Draw Os on the other piece. Cover the tagboard with clear contact paper.

3. Cut the Xs and Os into eighteen individual playing cards. To avoid crowding, make the playing cards slightly smaller than the sections of the master playing boards.

For a portable tic-tac-toe game, mount the master board inside a stationery box. Store the playing cards in the box.

GREEN IDEA • GREEN IDEA

# Cube-It

## Who

Preschoolers and schoolagers

## About the Toy

This activity gives children practice in counting objects from one to ten and matching the correct amount to each numeral. It also helps teach organizing by category, such as color, and emphasizes focusing on completing a specific task. The variation (on the following page) introduces the idea of completing a task quickly.

Two children can play this game, or it can be used by one child as an independent activity. The child spreads out all the task cards and reads the numerals or counts the dots to determine the number and color of blocks needed to complete the task. For example, if the number 4 has a red square, the child finds four red cubes and stacks them on that square. Use numbers 1 through 5 with younger children, saving the larger number sets for those who have mastered the first ones.

## What They Learn

Cognitive development skills: By the age of four, most children understand the meaning of numbers up to ten. They also understand the concept of cardinality—that the last word in a counting sequence indicates how many items are in a set. Giving young children frequent opportunities to expand and challenge their mathematical thinking, such as through age-appropriate math games involving counting and one-to-one correspondence, ensures a solid mathematical knowledge base, one that is essential for the variety of mathematical skills children will be taught in the years ahead.

## Extending the Learning

It has been said that mathematics is the only area of the curriculum with an identifiable "phobia" attached to it. If, however, a child's early experiences with math are positive, she is far less likely to develop a dislike of math in her later years. One way early childhood educators can help ensure children's math experiences are positive is to help children view math as asking (and answering!) questions about the world. For example, what are the shapes and patterns in nature? Why do spiders build their webs a certain way? Why are so many patterns in nature repeated? Early mathematical experiences that build on children's natural inquisitiveness about the world around them—that is, activities that are interesting and meaningful—will make learning abstract mathematical concepts later on much easier, not to mention more fun.

## What You Need

☐ tagboard sheets (8 by 10 inches each)

☐ black coding dots (optional)

☐ marker

☐ scissors

☐ clear contact paper

☐ construction paper

☐ ruler

☐ small stackable objects (such as color cubes, flat-surface beads, Lego building blocks, or small colored tagboard pieces)

## How to Make It

1. On one sheet of tagboard, rule off three or four rectangular work spaces and print a numeral at the left-hand side of each rectangle.

2. Mount the corresponding number of dots next to each numeral. (You can use the number 0; just leave the space empty). Make separate sets for numbers 1 through 5 and 6 through 10.

3. Cut 1-inch squares of construction paper in colors that match the color cubes you have. (For numbers from 6 through 10, provide two squares in each box.) Glue on the right-hand side of each rectangle.

4. Cover the counting boards with clear contact paper.

## Variation

For older children who like a special challenge, add a minute timer to see how quickly they can complete a card. Encourage the children to count their cubes as they stack them so they use the right quantity for each number.

Use chalk to create this game on the sidewalk. Children can use natural materials, such as small rocks and sticks, in place of the color cubes.

GREEN IDEA • GREEN IDEA

# Dominoes

## Who

Preschoolers and schoolagers

## About the Toy

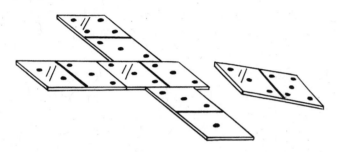

Two or more children can play this game (play with them at first to introduce the procedures). Have each child draw four to six dominoes from the basket. To begin, place one domino in the center, then take turns adding dominoes that match the number on the free side of the domino. A player who does not have a match can draw from the basket until a match comes up. If all the dominoes are used up and a player does not have a match, the next person who has a match continues. Continue playing until the dominoes are used up or no one can find a match. Count how many dominoes are in each row, if you wish. One child can also play this game as a matching activity.

## What They Learn

Cognitive development skills: Mathematical thinking, like literacy, develops through knowledge children acquire during everyday, informal learning experiences. Games with dominoes, for example, encourage paying attention to similarities and differences. Counting and matching skills are reinforced, as is skill with spatial relationships.

## Extending the Learning

Since play is the primary vehicle through which young children learn about their world, make sure that everyone has regular opportunities to engage in all types of play that are appealing to them. Types include games with rules, gross-motor games and activities, pretend play, and solitary play.

## What You Need

☐ two pieces of tagboard (8 by 11 inches each)

☐ small coding dots (black or another color)

☐ ruler

☐ marker

☐ scissors

☐ clear contact paper

☐ basket or box

## How to Make It

1. On each piece of tagboard, measure and mark off twelve rectangles, approximately 2 by 3 inches each, using dotted lines.

2. Draw a solid line through the middle of each rectangle, running from top to bottom (this line separates the domino into its two parts).

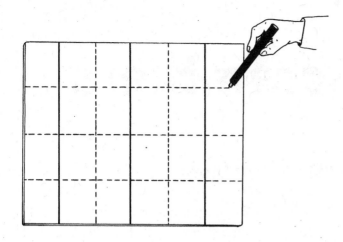

3. Place patterns of one to six coding dots on each side of the solid lines in each rectangle. Keep the patterns of dots consistent for each number.

4. Cover both sides of the tagboard with contact paper. Follow the dotted lines to cut out each domino.

5. Store the dominoes in a basket or box.

Instead of coding dots, create line drawings or cut photographs from magazines to make picture dominoes. Play in the same manner as described above.

GREEN IDEA • GREEN IDEA

# Wipe-Off Scramblers

## Who

Preschoolers and schoolagers

## About the Toy

Children can use these cards individually or as a small-group activity. Place the cards, washable markers, and damp sponges on a table. Have children draw lines to connect pictures that look alike. Watch for the children's ability to recognize likenesses and differences, and use harder or easier cards to match their ability levels. Call attention to details and identify characteristics in pictures to help children develop matching skills. When finished with one card, children take the sponge and wipe off the card.

Make several cards at different levels of difficulty and in various topics by using different stickers or pictures. You can also make cards to match letters, numbers, colors, or shapes or to teach other concepts, such as opposites or associations.

## What They Learn

Language and communication development skills: Formal reading instruction, such as phonics worksheets, is inappropriate for children between the ages of four and five, since most children this age do not have the neural development required for pencil-and-paper types of drills. There are, however, many appropriate prereading activities, such as noticing likenesses and differences on these wipe-off cards that help build a foundation for literacy.

## Extending the Learning

Reading comprehension is built on the associations children form throughout childhood from real experiences with the world. Literacy activities for preschoolers and schoolagers should be varied and focus on specific language and listening skills. The best predictor of later reading success, however, is the time spent reading to a child, so be sure to read to the children in your care every day.

## What You Need

☐ pairs of stickers or small pictures from magazines or workbooks (about ten per card)

☐ tagboard or index cards (5½ by 8 inches)

☐ markers or crayons

☐ small sponges in a bowl

☐ box or tray to hold materials

☐ clear contact paper

## How to Make It

1. Mount stickers in two parallel columns along the side of each piece of tagboard or index card. Leave about 2½ to 3 inches of space between the rows. (For very young children, place matching stickers within one to two spaces of each other.)

2. Make several different cards. Vary the difficulty by making some cards with slight differences and others with more obvious differences. Cover all of the cards with clear contact paper. You can also use resealable plastic bags for wipe-off cards.

3. Place the sets of cards and the markers, bowl, and sponges in the box or tray for easy use.

## Variations

The following are some additional topics for wipe-off cards:

**Things that go together:** hammer/nail, screwdriver/screw, saw/wood, key/lock, paint/paintbrush.

**Things we use:** toothbrush/toothpaste, fork/knife, brush/comb, mittens/winter hat, sand pail/shovel.

**Who would eat it?** child/toast, dog/bone, cow/grass, bear/honey, bird/worm.

**Who lives there?** spider/web, bee/hive, people/house, bird/nest, fish/goldfish bowl.

**Opposites:** up/down (teeter-totter), hot/cold (fire/ice), big/little (elephant/ant), fast/slow (airplane/turtle), sweet/sour (sugar/lemon), soft/hard (pillow/rock).

**Sports:** tennis racket/tennis ball, baseball bat/baseball, bowling pin/bowling ball, golf club/golf ball, hockey stick/hockey puck.

Resealable plastic bags can be hand washed and used multiple times.

# Cue Me In

## Who

Preschoolers and schoolagers

## About the Toy

This activity helps teach color, shape, and number recognition. Begin by putting the cue cards inside each child's decorated bag. Vary the number of cards (anywhere from one to ten) according to the ages and abilities of the children. Have children walk around the room or yard and collect items that match the cue cards. Here are samples of cue cards and their uses:

- colored strips of paper—children find matching colors
- shape cards—children find items of matching shapes
- cards with numerals (for example, the number 4 and the same number of dots—children collect four items)

Vary the cue cards in each child's bag so they each are looking for a different color or type of item. As the children get used to this game, or for older children, have the cue cards combine tasks. For example, have the children look for colors, shapes, and numbers, such as three square blocks or two red beads.

## What They Learn

Cognitive development skills: By the time children are four years old, they are able to perform many thinking tasks, such as grouping things by basic-level categories. For example, they can group similar furniture items such as chairs, beds, and tables. Most can also break things down into subcategories, such as separating rocking chairs from dining room chairs, which are both in the more general category *chairs*. This activity encourages children to use their categorization skills as they look for and match items that share similar characteristics.

## Extending the Learning

As children learn more about the world around them, their language skills and vocabularies increase—they have more to talk about! You can enhance children's learning during activities such as this one by asking children to talk about the items they find and collect. For example, ask a child, "What is on your card? A shape? What is the shape? A square. Where might you find things in the room that are shaped like squares?" Noticing specific characteristics and details of things in their environment is also an important prereading skill for children.

## What You Need

- [ ] paper bags
- [ ] unlined index cards
- [ ] scissors
- [ ] markers
- [ ] small coding dots
- [ ] construction paper of various colors

## How to Make It

1. Have children decorate their bags and put their names on them.

2. Cut small strips of construction paper for color cues. Cut a variety of shapes to use as combined shape and color cues for older children.

3. Make other cue cards by tracing or drawing a variety of shapes or objects on the index cards. Make several of each kind and place them in the bags.

4. To make number cue cards, write large numerals on the cards. For younger children, mount a matching number of dots next to the numeral.

## Variation

Consider making specialized cue cards for items in your outdoor environment, such as leaves, rocks, shells, flowers, and grass.

When the children have finished using the bags, you can use them for grocery shopping. Keep a few bags in your car for unplanned trips to the store.

# File-Folder Fun

## Who

Preschoolers and schoolagers

## About the Toy

Learning to recognize how different things are grouped together and to make associations about similarities and differences in words and concepts help build vocabulary and word usage skills. Sorting out and discussing the pictures encourage logical thinking and creative expression.

Encourage children to file or sort the picture cards into folders according to categories, such as clothes, toys, food, furniture, or things that fly. This game has unlimited possibilities since you can make up endless categories for the file folders, such as letter sounds, colors, shapes, and seasons. You can adapt the game to almost any theme and make it easier or harder depending on the type or complexity of categories you choose.

As the children file the pictures, encourage them to describe and tell stories about them. Count how many objects are in each file. Talk about what other objects they can think of that belong in these categories. Use the files on a table or the floor, hang them from a display rack (see p. 200), or use them as part of an office or some other dramatic play area.

## What They Learn

Language and communication development skills: Before children can learn to read, they must be able to grasp the concept that specific symbols, such as printed letters and words, and toy cars and dollhouses, correspond to specific things in their environment. Preschool and school-age children have the capacity to begin making these connections. Their rapidly expanding language skills and life experiences make it easier for them to make the mental leap from things in the real world to things they can imagine in their minds.

## Extending the Learning

In this activity, children recognize that the pictures (symbols) represent objects that have meaning, and that by sorting the pictures they are, in a sense, reading them. Once children understand the connection between one type of symbol and its real-world equivalent, it becomes easier for them to understand other symbol/real-world connections. Encouraging children to describe and tell stories about the cards as they file them will enhance this learning.

## What You Need

☐ pocket file folders

☐ stapler

☐ scissors

- ☐ cloth tape
- ☐ sources for pictures (such as old magazines or catalogs)
- ☐ unlined index cards (4 by 6 inches)
- ☐ glue stick
- ☐ marker
- ☐ clear contact paper
- ☐ large manila envelopes or box to store folders and file cards

## How to Make It

1. Cut the file folder in half and staple the pocket along both sides. Cover the stapled sides with cloth tape.

2. Cut out six or more pictures of items in each of several categories. (For example, food, clothing, vehicles, animals, or toys.)

3. Glue the pictures onto the index cards. Mount one picture from each category on each folder pocket and reinforce it by covering it with contact paper. Print the name of the category above the pocket near the top of the folder. (Older children will enjoy cutting out the pictures themselves and, with direction, can also glue them to the index cards.)

4. Cover the remaining file cards with contact paper and store them with the folders in the manila envelope or box.

## Variations

Sorting items by categories can be extended to include more complex associations or concepts:

| Category | Picture on Folder |
| --- | --- |
| Where would you find it? | things on land, in the sea, or in the air |
| Who would wear it or use it? | adult, child, or baby |
| Where does it go? | kitchen, bathroom, living room, or garage |
| What makes it go or move? | people, electricity, wind, or fuel/gas |

You can also use bulletin boards for sorting pictures, letting the children arrange the items into various categories. For example, create a bulletin board featuring pictures of a store. Label the shelves or sections of the store with specific categories. Older children can use large pushpins to put pictures of items onto the appropriate shelves or sections on the bulletin board.

Reuse lids from boxes or whole candy boxes as sorting trays, labeling them with pictures from each category. Children then sort the pictures into the appropriate groups.

GREEN IDEA • GREEN IDEA

# Lids Unlimited

## Who

Preschoolers and schoolagers

## About the Toy

This activity provides many opportunities for recognizing likenesses and differences; matching color, size, and shape; and categorizing. When used with cue cards, this toy provides a logical thinking activity that also encourages prereading and premath skills.

You can use the lids for many different matching games. Begin by using the lids to talk about how they are alike and different. Select two lids that are exactly alike. Add a third lid that is different from the others in some way and talk about how it is different. For example, begin with two small blue lids, add a large blue lid, and then discuss difference in size, or add a yellow lid and discuss difference in color. Have the children group the lids by a designated characteristic. Make cue cards to use with the lids. Have children select a card and match the lids to the correct circles.

The variations (on the following page) encourage creativity by using lids in designs or pictures. Younger children may enjoy just manipulating the lids, stacking them together, making towers or rows, or using them in fill-and-dump activities.

## What They Learn

Cognitive development skills: Before four- and five-year-old children can begin internalizing number concepts, they need a variety of concrete experiences with small objects they can hold and count. Early childhood educators call these kinds of objects *manipulatives*. Manipulatives are sets of objects, such as small blocks, beads, buttons, dried beans, and crayons, that can be easily counted. Even after they have mastered basic skills, such as counting to ten and one-to-one correspondence, children can still use manipulatives to help learn new mathematical concepts, such as addition and subtraction.

## Extending the Learning

In this activity, the plastic lids function as manipulatives. Manipulatives can be used for other math-related activities, too, such as matching, categorizing, sequencing, and patterning. Be sure to read the variations at the end of this activity and choose ones that best meet the ability levels and interests of the children in your care.

## What You Need

☐ assorted clean plastic lids

☐ construction paper

☐ pencil

☐ scissors

☐ index cards (5 by 8 inches)

☐ glue

☐ clear contact paper

☐ marker

☐ box or basket

## How to Make It

1. Clean the lids and tops and allow them to dry. Consider using lids from spice jars, or pump hair spray, liquid soap, and milk bottles.

2. Trace the lids onto construction paper of a matching color. Cut out many of each size and color.

3. To make cue cards, glue the circles onto the index cards in a variety of combinations. Also make some that give more specific directions for the children to follow. Cover the cue cards with clear contact paper.

4. Store the cue cards and lids in a basket or box.

## Variations

**Sequencing game:** Arrange the circles in sequences of size and color. Make many different sequences. Have the children match the lids to the sequences on the card. Let the children make up their own sequence patterns.

**Puzzle or picture completion:** Make cue cards that contain outlines of various things (animals, birds, or insects work well, as do pictures of snowmen or gingerbread men). Leave spaces for a lid or several lids to complete the picture. Encourage children to notice and talk about what size will complete the picture. Give the children some blank paper and let them draw their own pictures to complete.

**Design cards:** Use circle cutouts of all different colors and sizes to make various free-form design cards. Have the children cover the circles with lids to create three-dimensional designs.

**Following-directions game:** Use cue cards that give instructions to follow, such as, "Stack four lids" or "Put two blue pen tops in a yellow lid." Children follow directions on each card. Keep directions for younger children very simple. For older children, the directions can be more complicated. (For example, "Put three items in one top, four in another.")

Covering cards with clear contact paper can promote durability, but it isn't necessary for the success of the activity. Consider using the cards without covering them, and then recycle them when they are no longer usable.

GREEN IDEA · GREEN IDEA ·

# Nailboard Design

## Who

Preschoolers and schoolagers

## About the Toy

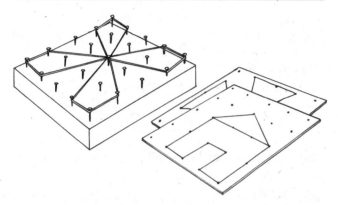

This activity stimulates creativity and imagination, teaches hand-eye coordination, and provides practice in using small-motor skills. When used with pattern cards, this activity can also help teach the children to follow directions and to count. The activity provides practice with manipulating sizes and shapes and with observing the sizes and characteristics of different shapes and sets of numbers.

Making the nailboards provides a fun project for schoolagers while teaching them woodworking skills, such as measuring, sanding, and pounding nails. It encourages them to follow a step-by-step process leading to a useful, completed product.

In this activity, children form different designs by stretching rubber bands from nail to nail. They can make up their own rubber band designs or they can try to follow patterns suggested by cue cards. You can also use the cue cards to prompt particular number tasks. (For example, "Make all the rubber bands go around four nails" or "How many sets of five nails can you enclose with the rubber bands?")

Encourage the children to experiment with different shapes (for example, trapezoid, parallelogram, pentagon) as they stretch their rubber bands in different formations, and then talk about them.

School-age children will enjoy making their own nailboards.

## What They Learn

Approaches to learning development skills: Creativity can be defined as the ability to create things that are original yet appropriate—things that others may not have thought of but that are useful in some way. Sometimes what a child creates opens up another child's way of thinking about something. Although creativity cannot be taught, certain personality characteristics or approaches to learning have been shown to foster creativity, for example, a willingness to take risks, patience, and persistence.

## Extending the Learning

Learning environments that promote experimentation and emphasize *process over product* are the ones in which children's creativity is most apt to flourish. Open-ended materials such as drawing tools and playdough naturally encourage more creativity and imagination. In this activity, it is important that children understand there is no right way to use the rubber bands. Asking the children questions while they work also fosters creative thinking and expressive language skills. For example, you might say, "You stretched two red rubber bands all the way across the piece of wood, and these four blue ones only half as far. What shape or picture are you making? Is it your very own design? Wow!"

## What You Need

- ☐ piece of wood (8 by 8 inches and 1 inch thick)
- ☐ sandpaper
- ☐ pencil
- ☐ ruler
- ☐ twenty-five 2-inch nails
- ☐ hammer
- ☐ rubber bands in assorted colors and sizes
- ☐ index cards (3 by 5 inches)

## How to Make It

1. Sand the wood to make sure it has no splinters or rough edges.

2. Measure and mark twenty-five dots on the board about 1¼ inches apart, starting 1 inch from the outer edges of the board (there should be five nails in each row). At each dot, hammer a nail about halfway into the board.

3. To make design cards to use with the nail-boards, draw patterns on the index cards using markers that are the same color as the rubber bands. Make shapes or simple objects that can be formed using straight lines, such as a house, a flag, or a zigzag pattern.

## Variation

Make larger boards using more nails. Boards with one hundred nails (ten rows of ten nails each) are useful for teaching number concepts.

Make sure that you use untreated wood in this activity. Treated wood contains chemicals that may be harmful to humans and animals.

GREEN IDEA · GREEN IDEA

# Banjo

## Who

Preschoolers and schoolagers

## About the Toy

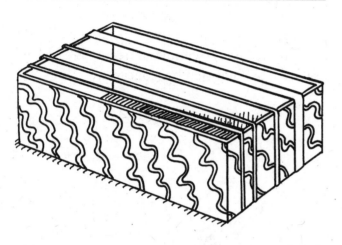

This banjo enhances enjoyment and appreciation of music and provides children with a means of actively participating in musical learning. The banjo focuses attention on some of the basic elements of music, such as tempo, rhythm, pitch, and quality of sound. It also offers a way of experimenting with the factors that help produce sound (vibration, tautness of string, thickness of string, size of open cavity). Children learn that the way an instrument is played (strumming versus plucking) can change the sound. Using this instrument can help teach children words such as *high, low, slow, resonance, vibration, pluck,* and *strum.*

Add several banjos to a rhythm band collection and let the children strum them during a music activity, or let children use them independently to accompany recorded music. Children can also use them as props in dramatic play.

Use the banjos to experiment with sound too. Vary the size of the boxes and the thickness of the rubber bands. Encourage the children to notice the effects of different combinations of rubber bands and different ways of playing them.

## What They Learn

Approaches to learning development skills: Most young children love music and any activities involving music. Exposure to music at an early age enhances children's learning by promoting creativity, coordination, language development, and social interaction. In addition, preschoolers and schoolagers will come to understand music and movement as a form of nonverbal communication as they discover that they can tell stories and express their feelings through their body movements.

## Extending the Learning

You don't need to play an instrument well or have a wonderful singing voice to help children appreciate musical sounds. Singing simple songs and chants or playing music that inspires children to twirl, leap, and clap their hands is all that's needed. Playing follow-the-leader movement games set to music and using props to help tell the story of a song are also activities four- and five-year-olds will enjoy. When you need to get the children's attention, try humming a tune that tells them you need them to stop what they're doing and join you. Make transition times more fun by creating your own lyrics to a tune the children all know. For example, to the tune of "Old MacDonald," you might sing, "Who would like to go outside? Antonio and Jo and Izzy. Who else will join us in this line? Jake, and Sam, and Rashid."

## What You Need

- [ ] sturdy rectangular boxes or plastic containers in various sizes (such as stationery boxes, shoeboxes, or plastic storage box lids that are 1½ to 2 inches deep)
- [ ] rubber bands of different thicknesses
- [ ] colorful contact paper (optional)
- [ ] scissors

## How to Make It

1. If you are using contact paper, cover the sides of selected containers with it.

2. Select three to six rubber bands of different thicknesses and stretch them around the longer dimension of the container. Arrange them in sequence from thin to thick (high to low sounds).

When the children have finished with the banjos, remove the rubber bands and use them and the boxes again in a different activity.

GREEN IDEA · GREEN IDEA

# Beautiful Beans, Nutritious Beans

## Who

Older preschoolers and schoolagers

## About the Toy

This activity helps children become aware of design in nature and how food can be enjoyed on different levels. They will learn the characteristics of one of the major food staples in the world. This activity will enhance language development, number skills, and the ability to follow directions. When the children make the soup, they will learn about the importance of preparation (learning to anticipate) and delayed gratification (waiting for the soup to finish cooking). The Beautiful Beans, Nutritious Beans jar makes a very nice family gift.

Layering the beans in a clear container is a way for children to manipulate materials into a design. For children who are working on following spatial directions, you might set out an example of a completed jar. When this activity is done as a creative project, briefly show an example, then put it away and encourage the children to make up their own designs—there are no right or wrong ways.

Children may examine how they layered their beans differently from someone else or whether they layered them in the same order. You might enhance the discussion by noting, "I see you and Tara both began with a layer of kidney beans and put a layer of black-eyed peas on top. Did you layer any of the other beans or legumes the same way?" For schoolagers who can read, label the beans and legumes and give them a list of the order they should place them in. Have labeled pictures available for basic research. The children may also help you or their families prepare a soup using the beans.

## What They Learn

Social and emotional development skills: Activities that involve food are great opportunities for children to try out and learn new social skills. Their learning is enhanced when an adult is involved, for example, by initiating conversations and modeling good manners. Mealtimes and snacktimes can also be used to teach children about healthy eating and healthy lifestyles. And, when an adult joins a group of children at a table to eat, it says to the children that the adult values their company and that all of their experiences are important.

## Extending the Learning

Since preschoolers and schoolagers are all about play, it is sometimes difficult for them to understand why mealtimes should be any different. Rather than focusing on what a child is doing wrong at the table, make a point of rewarding her good behavior. For example, saying, "Evan, slow down—don't grab the plate from Mei," you might say, "Evan, if you ask Mei to please pass you the plate, I think she will do it." Finally, if a child is having difficulty remaining at the table, simply excuse her and finish the meal with the remaining children.

## What You Need

### FOR THE BEAUTIFUL BEANS, NUTRITIOUS BEANS JAR:

☐ clear plastic jar with lid (one jar per child)

☐ a variety of beans (⅓ cup of each per child)

☐ ⅓-cup measuring cups

### FOR EIGHT-BEAN SOUP:

☐ 8-quart saucepan

☐ large bowl

☐ paring knife

☐ vegetable brush

☐ measuring cups

## How to Make It

1. Have the children clean and remove the labels from their jars. Dry them thoroughly.

2. Pour the beans into individual containers or roll the sides of a bag down for easy access by children. Consider using lentils, dried lima beans, black beans, white beans, kidney beans, and black-eyed peas. Community co-ops are generally the most inexpensive source of beans. Put the containers of beans and the measuring cups on a worktable.

3. Invite the children to scoop one type of bean into their measuring cup and empty the cup into the jar. Have them repeat the process, using the beans in any order they choose.

4. Cover the jar with its lid. Let the jars grace the room with their beauty awhile, and then either make soup or send the beans and the following recipe home with the children. Encourage parents and children to make the soup.

### EIGHT-BEAN SOUP

⅓ cup each of dried lima beans, black beans, white beans, kidney beans, and black-eyed peas

½ cup each of lentils, yellow split peas, green split peas, and barley

3 quarts cold water

one large onion, chopped

three large carrots, chopped

three stalks of celery with leaves, chopped

one bay leaf

a few grains of crushed red pepper (optional)

one 28-oz. can Italian plum tomatoes with juice, chopped

2 Tbsp. chopped fresh basil, or 1½ tsp. dried, crushed basil

salt and pepper to taste

5. Place all the beans together and wash them thoroughly. Add enough water to cover them, and soak them overnight. Drain well. Add the beans and 3 quarts of fresh water to an 8-quart saucepan.

6. Add the onion, carrots, celery, bay leaf, and red pepper (if desired) to the beans. Bring to a boil. Simmer for two hours or until the beans are almost soft.

7. Add the tomatoes and cook until the beans are well done. Add the basil, salt, and pepper just before serving.

Take a field trip to a local farm or farmer's market. If neither of these trips is possible, visit a local grocery store and talk about where the food items come from.

# Binoculars

## Who

Preschoolers and schoolagers

## About the Toy

After creating the binoculars, children can take them along on outdoor walks and use them to pretend to study or look at things in the distance, just as people do with real binoculars. Talk about where and how people use binoculars—such as on safari, for bird watching, or at sporting events and the opera—and encourage children to create some of these situations in dramatic play.

With a little adult assistance, older children can make the binoculars by themselves.

## What They Learn

Sensory perception development skills: These binoculars can be used in a variety of activities that will help children become more aware of how they use their eyes. Because the binoculars screen out the periphery, they are helpful in showing children how to focus on a particular object. Children can use the binoculars to observe and explore many things close up in both indoor and outdoor environments.

## Extending the Learning

Talk with the children about how people use binoculars outdoors, such as on nature walks or to spot birds, animals, and natural features from a distance. If binoculars are available, consider showing children what they look like and how to use them. Indoors, have children use the toy binoculars to go on a shape search by finding items that are shaped like circles, squares, rectangles, and triangles, or invite the children to use the binoculars to look around the classroom for specific colors.

## What You Need

☐ toilet paper tubes (two tubes per binocular)

☐ thin ribbon, elastic, or shoelaces
    (about 2 to 2½ feet long)

☐ contact paper or construction paper
    (two 5-by-6-inch pieces per binocular)

☐ tape

☐ stapler

☐ hole punch

## How to Make It

1. Cover each tube with the paper. Cut the pieces of paper slightly larger than the tubes to allow

for thorough coverage and easy taping. Staple the tubes together at the top and bottom.

2. Punch holes on the outer sides of the toilet paper tubes, about 1 inch from the top. Thread the ribbon, elastic, or shoelaces through the holes for a neck band. To secure the neck band, tie a knot at both ends so it can't slip out through the holes or staple it to each side.

> If you have short pieces of ribbon or elastic, tie them together to make a length long enough for a neck band.

# Gas Pump

## Who

Preschoolers and schoolagers

## About the Toy

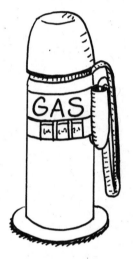

This activity provides children with something they can make and use in their play. You also can create gas pumps to use in connection with a field trip to a service station or in studying about transportation. Making pumps can also stimulate ideas for block building. Constructing the pumps uses small-motor skills and provides practice in planning and following directions. It offers an example of transforming common objects into props to use in imaginative play.

This is an excellent project for older preschoolers and schoolagers to create by themselves. Collect several toothpaste pumps and ask the children to think of things to make from them (for example, rockets or silos). Show the materials for making a gas pump as well. Discuss ways of attaching the parts. Let the children make the things they'd like to make. Encourage them to help one another, and assist as needed. Use the children's creations in the block corner when they're building cities and roads. The gas pumps can also be used with small cars to "fill 'er up!"

## What They Learn

Social and emotional development skills: The play of four- and five-year-olds is very different from the play of three-year-olds and toddlers. At this age, children's play is less associated with real-life situations and conditions and involves much more make-believe play. Initially, pretend play is directed toward the self. Eventually, children begin constructing make-believe scenarios involving other children as well as incorporating toys and other props into their games. Young children's make-believe has many benefits. For example, sometimes this type of play allows a child to revisit an anxiety-causing event, such as a trip to the doctor's office, by taking control and working through the event so that it no longer causes him to feel anxious.

## Extending the Learning

Much of the time, adults watch children's pretend play from a distance, occasionally picking up bits and pieces of the children's interactions. Sometimes, however, you may be asked to join in the play. If you do, resist the temptation to take charge. Instead, take an active role but use it as a way to enhance children's play rather than direct it. You can learn a great deal about a child's level of development as well as his thoughts by asking open-ended questions that are a natural part of the make-believe experience. For example, if you are a gas-station attendant, ask a child, "What kind of gasoline does your car take? How much gasoline do you need? Are you going on a long trip? Where are you going?"

## What You Need

- ☐ pump toothpaste container
- ☐ construction paper
- ☐ scissors
- ☐ pen cap with a clip
- ☐ shoelace
- ☐ glue stick
- ☐ cellophane tape
- ☐ marker

## How to Make It

1. Cut pieces of construction paper to fit around the toothpaste pump, allowing overlap for easy gluing. Wrap the paper around the pump and glue in place.

2. Attach the pen cap just above the middle of the pump by running tape around the pump and through the plastic or metal clip on the cap. Be sure the cap opening faces up.

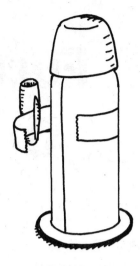

3. Cut the shoelace in half (so it is 12 to 14 inches in length) and tape it to the pump above the pen cap. Run the tape around the pump and around the cut end of the lace.

4. Decorate the pump with markers. Print the word *gas* and draw dials and numbers on the pump. Affix the tip of the shoelace to the pen cap.

## Variation

Make larger gas pumps using thin, tall cartons, thin plastic tubing for the hose, and handles from pump spray bottles. You can use a plastic or paper cup with a handle to hold the nozzle. Attach all of the parts with duct tape.

Ask area dentists if you can set up a used pump toothpaste collection box. Once a month or so, you can pick up the pump toothpaste containers and use them with the children.

GREEN IDEA · GREEN IDEA

# Furry Animals/ 3-D Friends

## Who

Preschoolers and schoolagers

## About the Toy

This activity serves as a good model of making and using homemade toys. For example, schoolagers can make and keep these play figures themselves or give them as gifts to siblings or friends. Families can get involved by collecting materials for the stuffed animals (such as magazine or catalog pictures), and you can provide them with instructions on how to make the play figures.

Children can also use the figures as props in dramatic play, for example, by using several bears to have a teddy bears' picnic or act out the story *The Three Bears*.

## What They Learn

Social and emotional development skills: As a child's language skills increase, she is more able to regulate her emotions as well as to take others' emotional perspectives. Empathy becomes an important motivator for preschool and school-age children in learning prosocial, or altruistic, behavior—that is, behavior that benefits someone else without the expectation of any kind of reward. This does not, however, mean that four- and five-year-olds can necessarily sympathize with or be concerned about someone else's situation. These types of prosocial behaviors can be confusing for children this age, and developing them fully takes time.

## Extending the Learning

Adults can help foster children's emotional understanding by acknowledging and explaining emotional reactions as they occur. Dialogues of this kind enable young children to transfer what they learn about emotions to other contexts, such as in conversations with siblings and friends, and during make-believe play with other children. With time, children learn that recognizing others' emotions as well as being able to explain their own, enhances the relationships they have with their family and friends. In addition, community service or other activities in which children give goods or services to others promotes altruism. For example, consider having schoolagers make and give these toys to children who do not receive gifts very often.

## What You Need

- ☐ a picture (about 8½ by 11 inches)
- ☐ scissors
- ☐ clear contact paper
- ☐ material for the back of the figure (such as fake fur for animals, or shiny plastic or fabric for 3-D figures)
- ☐ a resealable plastic bag approximately the same size as the picture
- ☐ cotton batting or foam pieces
- ☐ stapler

## How to Make It

1. Cut out a picture of an animal toy or a storybook or TV character.

2. Place the contact paper sticky side up on a flat surface. Center the picture face down on the contact paper and press to smooth. Trim the edges with scissors.

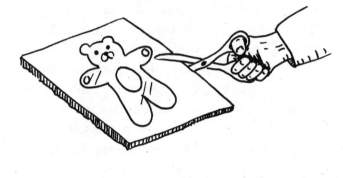

3. Place the animal figure on the fake fur (fur side down), trace around it, and cut it out. Place other characters on fabric or plastic in the same way.

4. Stuff cotton batting or foam pieces into the plastic bag. Fill to approximately 1½ inches thick. (Putting the stuffing in a plastic bag makes the assembly process much easier.)

5. Put the three pieces together: animal picture on one side, fur cutout (fur side out) on the other, and stuffed bag in the middle. Staple or sew around the edges. If the toy is for toddlers, punch holes around the animal and lace or sew it shut (toddlers can pull out staples). School-agers, however, enjoy using a stapler and will be more successful at it.

Ask fabric stores for donations of fake fur scraps.

# Quick-and-Easy Doll Clothes

## Who

Preschoolers and schoolagers

## About the Toy

Children can use these clothes for dressing and undressing dolls. Have the children practice mixing and matching outfits made from various colored socks. Socks are easy for the children to pull on and off because they stretch and because no buttons are involved. Children also can wash the clothes and use clothespins to hang them on lines to dry.

Schoolagers can make the clothes themselves, decorating them with bits of lace, glitter, appliqué, and other additions. Make various sizes of clothes by using a variety of sock sizes. Socks really stretch, so even small ones can be used to make usable outfits for small dolls.

## What They Learn

Physical and motor development and language and communication development skills: Even though children this age are capable of dressing and undressing themselves, many will still enjoy practicing the fine-motor skills involved in making and decorating doll clothes, and they enjoy dressing and undressing dolls. Their language skills are also enhanced when they describe their actions to other children while they work.

## Extending the Learning

Use your knowledge of the children to anticipate which steps in the process of making the doll clothes they may need help with. Sewing the socks is likely to be one of them. In general, it is always best to allow children to perform any tasks they are capable of performing. There is satisfaction in creating something all on one's own, and self-efficacy and self-esteem are enhanced as well. Asking children open-ended questions about their creations promotes language skills and vocabulary. For example, ask a child, "What item of clothing are you making? Will you decorate it? What will you use to decorate it? Which doll will wear that skirt?" You also can use this activity to discuss the care of clothes, such as washing and folding them.

## What You Need

☐ socks
☐ scissors

□ needle and thread

□ decorations (such as fabric paint, lace, and appliqué)

□ fabric glue

## How to Make It

1. Cut a sock into thirds, separating the toe section, the middle heel portion, and the top.

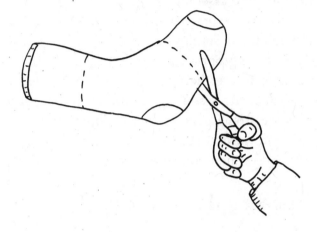

2. Use the top of the sock for a dress or shirt. Cut out arm holes on either side.

3. Use the midsection for shorts or pants. Sew a small closing in the middle of one end to provide the separation for legs. To create long pants, cut an arch shape in one end and sew the edges closed. Fold up the edges of the toe section to make a hat.

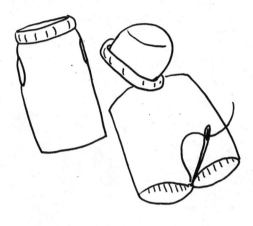

4. Decorate as desired.

This is a great way to use socks that no longer have a match.

# Take-Apart People

## Who

Preschoolers and schoolagers

## About the Toy

Children take these dolls apart and put them together. Older children will be challenged by fitting the dolls together and manipulating the fasteners.

Demonstrate how to assemble the doll and call attention to the way the arms and legs are attached when the doll is assembled correctly. Have the children look at their own hands and feet and notice where their thumbs and toes point.

Older children may want to cut out or make doll clothes. For younger children, attach Velcro to the dolls and clothes for easy changes. Use the doll in connection with different topics by changing its outfits.

## What They Learn

Physical and motor development and language and communication development skills: These paper dolls can be used for a variety of activities appropriate for four- and five-year-olds. When children help make the dolls by tracing patterns, cutting out the dolls, and assembling the dolls with brass fasteners, they are practicing small-muscle coordination. Children develop recognition of body parts and learn appropriate placement by noticing, for example, where their thumbs and toes point as they attach arms and legs to the dolls. Language skills are strengthened when children talk about ideas and words associated with their own bodies, such as how their body parts function and move.

## Extending the Learning

Children will use these dolls differently, depending on their interests and developmental levels. As children help create the dolls, encourage them to give the dolls different facial expressions and use this as an opportunity to discuss different emotions. Ask a child, "How can you draw this doll's face to show that he's happy? Will his mouth turn up at the corners or point down?" "What would an excited expression look like?" Older children may enjoy designing and making paper clothes for the dolls.

## What You Need

☐ patterns for arms, legs, torso, head, and wigs

☐ tagboard

☐ pencil

☐ markers

☐ scissors

☐ clear contact paper

☐ Velcro

- ☐ hole punch
- ☐ brass fasteners, twist ties from bags, or Velcro
- ☐ material for doll clothes (such as fabric, colored plastic, or wallpaper samples)
- ☐ shoebox or resealable plastic bags

## How to Make It

1. Trace patterns on tagboard for the torso and limbs. Make your own patterns or use patterns from paper-doll books.

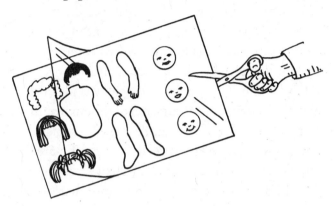

2. Show cultural diversity by making a variety of hair types and styles and coloring the dolls in various skin tones. Make several different facial expressions on a number of the heads. Cover the parts with contact paper and cut them out. Add a small piece of Velcro to the tops of heads and backs of hair samples.

3. Punch holes in the body parts. Use fasteners or ties to attach the limbs and head to the torso. (It is better to use Velcro for younger children, but using it means body parts will not move.)

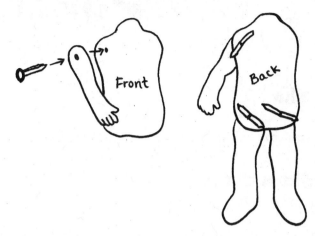

4. Make a variety of doll clothes for various occupations, seasons, and activities. Punch holes in the clothes so they fit over the brass fasteners, or attach Velcro to the doll and clothes. Store the dolls and outfits in shoeboxes or resealable plastic bags.

Dolls don't require water, but humans do. Be aware of how you use water. If necessary, change your habits to lessen the amount of water you use unnecessarily: turn off the water while you brush your teeth, repair any leaking faucets, and, if you need to water outdoor plants, use a watering can rather than a hose.

GREEN IDEA · GREEN IDEA ·

# Puzzlemania

## Who

Preschoolers and schoolagers

## About the Toy

This puzzle introduces the concept of spatial relations by calling attention to shape as a tool in working on a puzzle. It also sharpens visual-perception and small-motor skills.

Create instant puzzles using found objects of all sorts. Place the outline master playing board and the items that go with it on a table and let the children find the pieces that fit into the individual outlines.

Schoolagers will enjoy tracing around the objects to make these puzzles. Encourage the children to notice what the outline of an item looks like. See if they can identify the item by looking at the outline before trying the pieces. Notice that some things with irregular or specific shapes (such as a paper clip or a fork) are easy to identify whereas a square shape could be many different items.

With older children, discuss the concept of dimension (the outlines are two-dimensional and the real objects are three-dimensional) and how that affects what things look like.

## What They Learn

Cognitive development skills: Among the physical-knowledge skills children this age are working to acquire are spatial skills. *Spatial skills* refers to the ability to perceive the visual-spatial world accurately. Young children develop spatial skills through active and physical exploration of the environment. For young children, toys and other experiences that don't appear to relate directly to specific areas of curriculum, such as math and science, are far more beneficial than educational software, workbooks, or other more traditional teaching tools.

## Extending the Learning

For children to form concepts of the physical world, they need to get the feel of objects and their relationships in space, such as through manipulating puzzle pieces to see how they fit together. Children learn the concept of dimension when they can compare an outline (two-dimensional) to its real-life (three-dimensional) representation. Everyday experiences of climbing and crawling through things also help children learn about relationships in space, direction, and distance.

## What You Need

☐ tagboard

☐ assortment of objects with different shapes

☐ markers

□ clear contact paper

□ container

□ Velcro

## How to Make It

1. Select six to eight clean objects. Consider using cookie cutters, plastic silverware, block shapes, small toys, discarded puzzle pieces, keys, rubber bands, chalk, or old combs.

2. Trace each shape onto the tagboard. Use a 12-by-18-inch piece of tagboard for larger puzzles.

3. Cover the tagboard with contact paper. Place the objects in a container. When making multiple puzzles, color code the back of the tagboard and the container of objects that goes with it.

## Variations

For portable puzzles, trace the objects on a box top (such as one from a stationery or candy box) or mount tagboard on a box top. Keep the matching objects in the box. For a traveling puzzle, attach Velcro to the objects and to the matching spot on the outline on the box lid.

To make an outdoor version of this puzzle, use chalk to trace objects (such as leaves, rocks, branches, or plants) on the sidewalk.

This puzzle provides an easy-to-make activity that creatively reuses readily available materials. This, in turn, encourages the children to think about using commercial toys to create new games.

GREEN IDEA • GREEN IDEA

# Target Toss

## Who

Preschoolers and schoolagers

## About the Toy

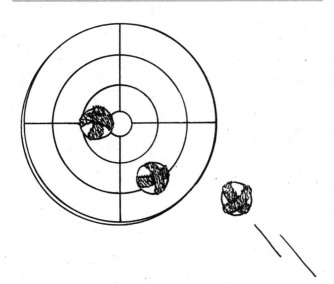

In this activity, children practice following directions and develop visual-motor skills. For older children, the activity provides practice in making up games and the accompanying rules. Mount stationary targets on walls, either indoors or out. Use Velcro patches for easy relocation. These targets can be used by individual children or by small teams playing together.

## What They Learn

Physical and motor development skills: In addition to developing fine-motor and gross-motor skills, preschoolers and schoolagers also begin developing skill-related, or performance-related, fitness abilities. Ball-handling skills such as tossing, throwing, and catching fall in the category of skill-related fitness abilities. Simple tossing and catching activities help strengthen hand-eye coordination as children learn to control the force of their tosses as well as to watch and predict how a ball will move through space as they learn to catch it.

## Extending the Learning

This activity fosters skill-related fitness abilities in a simple, nonthreatening environment. Be sure to demonstrate for children how to gently toss the balls at the wall targets. Explain how easily the balls stick and show them the best place to aim the balls (the middle area). Younger children may simply enjoy attaching and detaching balls from the target. Older children may enjoy more complicated games in which some children move while holding the targets and other children toss the balls at the moving targets. Target games with this toy are also good opportunities for older children to gain practice playing games with rules, including following directions and working together as a team.

## What You Need

☐ fabric panels (such as Velcro fabric, flannel, nubby wool, or jersey fabrics)

☐ heavy tape or staples

☐ scissors

☐ Velcro strips

☐ Nerf balls or old socks

## How to Make It

1. Cut the fabric panels to the desired target shape and size. Use heavy tape or staples to secure the fabric to a wall or the back side of shelving.

2. Make fabric balls from old socks rolled up and wadded inside themselves. Wrap 1½- to 2-inch lengths of Velcro around the fabric balls or other small balls. (Test to make sure Velcro sticks to the fabric panel.)

Save any fabric scraps for another toy or activity. For ideas see the Reusable and Donated Materials Index on pages 221–22.

GREEN IDEA · GREEN IDEA ·

# Sizzling Rockets

## Who

Preschoolers and schoolagers

## About the Toy

These rockets are a fun craft activity to make and use in connection with flight or rocket-themed units. Assemble the materials and assist the children as needed. Older preschoolers and schoolagers can make these toys as a craft activity related to learning about rockets or for experimenting with air, motion, and flight. Children can whirl them around in the air (inside or outside) and watch their rockets sparkle and flash and their tails sizzle as they whirl around.

Children can also launch their rockets by slipping them over a thin tube, dowel, or ruler and making a motion similar to an overhand throw. The rocket will fly off the launching device, traveling several yards before landing. It is best to launch the rockets outside or in a gym, where children can practice seeing how far their rockets will go.

## What They Learn

Approaches to learning development skills: Craft activities for young children present many learning opportunities. For example, the various craft materials used in this activity encourage tactile experiences and creative exploration. By following a project through from beginning to end, children show self-direction, independence, and persistence in completing tasks. In addition, the more open-ended the craft project is, the more likely children are to apply their knowledge in new ways and use multiple strategies for solving problems.

## Extending the Learning

These rocket toys can be used inside or outside and can help children learn about rockets, flight, air, and motion. While children construct their rockets, they can discuss the assembly process, including parts, shapes, and appearance. Playing with the rockets provides practice in running and throwing, two basic physical-activity skills children this age need to develop. Running with and flying the rockets helps develop coordinated body movements.

## What You Need

- ☐ toilet paper tubes
- ☐ shiny Mylar (6-by-10-inch pieces)
- ☐ scissors
- ☐ cellophane tape
- ☐ hole punch
- ☐ string (cut into 2- to 2½-foot pieces)
- ☐ thin cardboard tubes (such as from plastic wrap), dowels, round pillar type blocks, or rulers, to use as launchers

## How to Make It

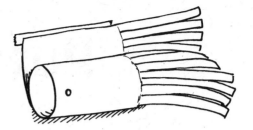

1. Fold the Mylar in half lengthwise. Open and fringe half of it, making cuts about ½ inch apart and 5 inches long (to the fold line).

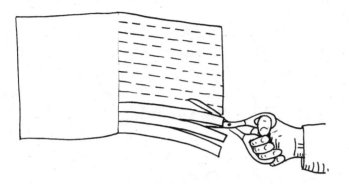

2. Cover the toilet paper tubes with the Mylar so one end is flush with the end of the tube and the fringe extends beyond the other end. Secure with tape.

3. Punch a hole approximately 1 inch from the unfringed end of the tube. Loop the string through the hole and tie. (You may staple the string to the tube, but you should also tie a knot in the string to prevent it from slipping through the staples.)

4. Hold the end of the string and whirl the tube around, turning and twisting it for added motion and effect. Children can launch their rockets by slipping them over a thin tube, dowel, or ruler and making a motion similar to an overhand throw.

> When the children have finished with the rockets, take them apart and reuse or recycle the parts. For example, save the Mylar and use it again for other activities.

GREEN IDEA · GREEN IDEA ·

# Puzzle Fix-It

## Who

Preschoolers and schoolagers

## About the Toy

This activity helps save money by providing a way to extend the usefulness of puzzles after a piece has been lost. Demonstrate the process of mixing the wood putty, lining the empty puzzle space with plastic wrap, and filling it in with wood putty. Discuss what can be done when the piece dries (such as sanding the edges and painting or coloring the piece to match the puzzle). You can also use this activity in a dramatic play fix-it shop.

## What They Learn

Social and emotional development skills: From their experiences in different settings, children begin to make judgments about their own worth and to construct feelings associated with those judgments—that is, they develop self-esteem. Because of its effect on so many of life's experiences, both present and future, self-esteem is among the most important aspects of a child's social and emotional development.

## Extending the Learning

Even simple activities such as helping repair puzzle pieces can leave children feeling good about themselves and their abilities. By extending an item's usefulness, children learn about caring for and maintaining items. Repairing an item and extending its usefulness can foster a can-do attitude and a confidence in one's own abilities and skills. Providing a child with a variety of experiences that help build his self-esteem and feelings of competence is one of the best ways of ensuring future learning success.

## What You Need

☐ puzzles with missing pieces

☐ wood putty

☐ plastic wrap

☐ acrylic paints

☐ small paintbrushes

☐ medium grade sandpaper

☐ spoon

## How to Make It

1. Complete the puzzle. Line the opening where the puzzle piece is missing with plastic wrap. Allow the plastic wrap to overlap an inch or more on all sides of the opening.

2. Fill the plastic-lined opening with putty so the putty fits completely around all of the sides and is level with the rest of the puzzle.

3. Let the putty dry completely (usually twenty-four hours). When it is dry, lift it up by the edges of the plastic wrap and remove the dried piece.

4. Sand the edges of the piece that feel uneven or do not fit smoothly. Paint the piece to match the puzzle.

This activity encourages schoolagers to care for and repair materials by giving them an opportunity to make and replace something that was lost. Making replacement pieces allows puzzles to stay complete and prevents puzzles with missing pieces from being thrown away.

# Desert in a Jar

## Who

Preschoolers and schoolagers

## About the Toy

Preschoolers and schoolagers can create a desert environment in a jar, and they can help collect sand and rocks for their terrariums. Encourage the children to observe how cacti and other desert plants are different from most houseplants.

When the children have completed their desert gardens and their study of desert plants, they can give the gardens to family members and impress them with their knowledge.

## What They Learn

Approaches to learning development skills: Young children are naturally curious and interested in exploring new things and novel situations. Activities involving nature capture children's attention because they help satisfy some of their curiosity

and they allow for freedom of exploration. In addition, nature activities provide opportunities for children to gain an understanding of and appreciation for the natural world, including the importance of Earth becoming a greener planet.

## Extending the Learning

This activity introduces children to some of the wonders of desert environments. Children unfamiliar with deserts will gain further understanding of the differences among the biomes of the earth, including weather, plants, and animals. Children's language skills are enhanced through desert-related discussions, such as why cacti are so prickly, how old they are and how big they grow, and whether or not any animals like to eat them. Be sure to provide different types of reference materials so children can discover the answers to their questions.

## What You Need

- ☐ jar
- ☐ sand
- ☐ small rocks
- ☐ small cactus plants
- ☐ tongs
- ☐ hammer and nail

## How to Make It

1. Wash and remove the label from a jar. Any large, wide-mouth, plastic jar with a lid will work (glass jars will work, but plastic is safer). Add 2 to 3 inches of sand to the bottom of the

jar. Using tongs, make shallow dents in the sand where cactus plants will be placed.

2. With tongs, carefully place the cacti into the dents. Drop in some small rocks. If necessary, arrange the rocks with the tongs.

3. Sprinkle just enough water into the jar to wet the sand. For continuing care, add water *only* when no beads of water moisture can be seen on the inside of the jar.

4. With the hammer and nail, make small holes in the lid. Screw the lid onto the jar.

Add plants to the children's environment. Plants add beauty and clean indoor air. Make sure all plants are nonpoisonous.

GREEN IDEA · GREEN IDEA ·

# Hanging Planter

## Who

Preschoolers and schoolagers

## About the Toy

This activity creates an attractive planter you can add to a science area to teach children about the care of plants and how certain aspects of the weather affect the crops that farmers grow.

Children can help fill these planters with dirt, learn how to plant seeds or transplant seedlings, and learn how to care for the plants. Younger children can observe how plants grow, such as how they grow toward the light. Older schoolagers might do some simple experiments, such as noting how different amounts of water or light can affect how the plants thrive. This can lead to discussions on the importance of rain during growing seasons.

Children can braid yarn for hanging the planter or make plastic bases for keeping the planters stable on a windowsill.

## What They Learn

Approaches to learning development skills: Some research suggests that regular play in natural environments has many developmental benefits for children. For example, children who play outdoors regularly show more advanced motor fitness, including balance and coordination. Their play also tends to be more diverse, imaginative, and creative, which fosters communication and cooperation skills. In addition, exposure to nature improves children's cognitive development by improving their awareness, reasoning, and observational skills.

## Extending the Learning

This activity helps children develop knowledge of plants and how they grow. To expand on their learning, talk with children about gardens and the various plants we eat from gardens as well as the importance of eating fruits and vegetables that are nutritious and good for our bodies. If possible, consider planting a small garden with the children and tending it throughout the seasons.

## What You Need

☐ plastic water bottles with caps

☐ marker

☐ knife or scissors

- ☐ yarn
- ☐ potting soil
- ☐ crushed rock
- ☐ seeds or small plants
- ☐ plastic trays (1 to 2 inches deep)

## How to Make It

1. Place the bottle on its side and draw a rectangular shape in the center. Using the knife or scissors, cut out a large opening along the lines.

2. Poke holes through the bottle, one on the short side of each opening (holes should be directly across from one another). Braid yarn and thread it through the holes. Tie large knots on each end of the yarn to secure it to the bottle.

3. Fill the bottom of the planter with crushed rock for drainage. Add dirt and sow seeds according to package directions or plant small plants. Place the planter in a well-lit area and add water regularly.

4. To create a stand for placing the planter on a windowsill, turn over a plastic tray and cut an oval hole down the center. This hole will support the middle section of the bottle. Place the planter into the stand.

Plastic water bottles can be recycled, but more often than not they end up in landfills, where they will never fully decompose. Ask for donations of used water bottles and be sure to empty and recycle them when the children are finished using them for this activity.

# Pulleys for Work and Play

## Who

Preschoolers and schoolagers

## About the Toy

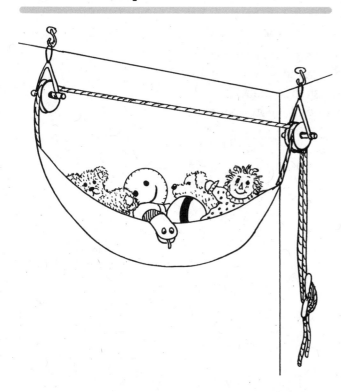

Pulleys introduce children to another way to use wheels. They help children learn about physics through hands-on experience. This activity promotes language development as you and the children discuss the components of pulleys, how they work, and the different ways people can use them. Pulleys encourage schoolagers to use their imaginations as they figure out different uses for them, and they promote large- and small-motor coordination, problem-solving skills, and scientific experimentation.

There are two options for this activity—homemade pulleys and working pulleys. A homemade pulley will not support much weight, but it can be used much like a clothesline for drying paintings or doll clothes or to support a basket for messages or other small, light items. In this system, two homemade pulleys are used at either end of a continuous loop of rope. The second option, working pulleys, requires store-bought pulleys, which can support more weight. One working pulley can be set up very simply, with a bucket or basket on one end of the rope to raise or lower toys from a loft, for example. Two working pulleys can be used in the same clothesline-type system as the homemade ones—that is, at either end of a continuous loop of rope—and used to move heavier items like a bird feeder or buckets of sand or water outside. You can set up three pulleys to raise and lower a hammock or net full of soft toys, as in the example below.

To introduce children to the use of the wheel, one of the three basic machines (a lever and the inclined plane are the other two), make a simple homemade pulley toy out of things from around the house or purchase pulleys at a hardware store.

Schoolagers can gather the materials needed to make the simple pulleys and can help construct them. They can also help figure out how to raise and lower a hammock or other storage container using several pulleys and some clothesline.

Explain to the preschoolers that pulleys are just wheels that help make lifting and moving things easier. For example, pulleys help make our cars run and make it possible to lift heavy steel beams to the top of tall buildings. Ask the children if they know of any other ways pulleys are working in their environment (for example, on Venetian blinds or elevators).

## What They Learn

Cognitive development skills: Simply defined, physics is the science of matter and energy and the interactions between the two. Physics activities for children, which usually involve the movement of objects, foster children's inquiry and problem-solving skills. According to Piaget's theory of cognitive development, children learn about physical properties in their environment by acting on objects and observing the objects' reactions. When children construct knowledge by acting on their environment, their understanding expands, which in turn contributes to their cognitive development.

## Extending the Learning

Curiosity and wonder are important motivators for lifelong learning. Hands-on physics activities, such as this one involving pulleys, promote scientific questioning and theory building. Be sure to explain to children how pulleys are used and why—to help lift things and make moving things easier. Older preschoolers and schoolagers can be encouraged to discuss the components of the pulleys, how they work, and the different ways people use them. Encourage all of the children to use their imaginations by considering different uses for the pulleys too.

## What You Need

### HOMEMADE PULLEYS

☐ two heavy-duty wire clothes hangers

☐ two empty metal or plastic adhesive tape reels (such as those used for medical purposes)

☐ glue

☐ pliers

☐ two ½-inch-diameter dowels (each 12 to 15 inches long)

☐ rope

☐ four rubber bands

☐ ice cream bucket

☐ clothespins (for hanging doll clothes or paintings)

## How to Make It

### HOMEMADE PULLEYS

1. Bend up the bottom of the hanger to form an upside down V shape. With the pliers, bend the hook of the hanger to make a closed loop.

2. Lay the dowel into one curve or "arm" of the hanger. Slip the reel onto the dowel, then lay the dowel into the other curve or "arm" so each end rests in one "arm" of the hanger.

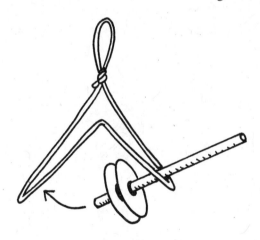

3. Place a rubber band on each end of the dowel near the hanger and apply glue (this keeps the dowel from slipping off the hanger).

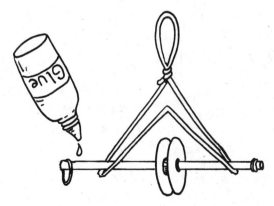

4. Repeat steps one through three to make a second pulley.

5. Suspend the hangers at the same height and far enough apart so that the children can see the pulley action. If you want a temporary clothesline, you could hang one end on a doorknob and the other on the back of a chair, for example.

6. Measure a straight line from one of the reels to the other to determine how far apart they are. Cut a piece of rope or clothesline twice that distance plus a foot.

7. If you want an ice cream bucket or a basket on the line for sending messages or small items, tie it in the middle of the line.

8. Feed the rope around both reels, pull it snug, and tie the ends together to form a continuous loop. If you've tied a basket onto the rope, make sure the basket is on the bottom of the loop. If you're going to use the line for hanging doll clothes or paintings, add clothespins.

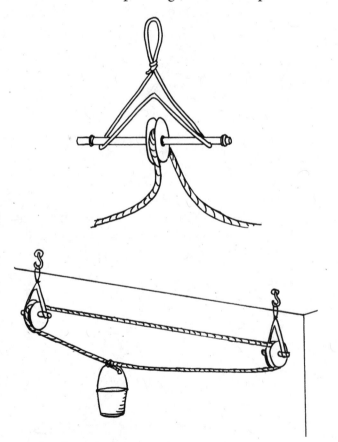

## What You Need

### WORKING PULLEY SYSTEM

☐ two 1-inch pulleys, one single and one double (a double pulley has two wheels and can accommodate two ropes)

☐ one cleat

☐ rope or clothesline

☐ two hooks

☐ doll-size hammock or net

## How to Make It

### WORKING PULLEY SYSTEM

1. Measure the length of the hammock. Attach two hooks to the ceiling or high up on the wall the same distance apart as the length of the hammock. Be sure the hooks are anchored into studs or joists so they will be strong enough to hold the weight of the hammock.

2. Fasten a cleat to a wall directly below or in line with one of the hooks. Make sure the cleat is within the children's reach.

3. Hang the double pulley on the hook above the cleat. Hang the single pulley on the other hook.

4. Measure two lengths of rope. The length of the first rope has to be twice the distance from the floor to the pulley. The length of the second rope must be twice the distance from the floor to the pulley plus the distance between the two pulleys.

5. Lay the hammock on the floor. Tie the shorter rope to one end of the hammock and the longer rope to the other end. Thread the shorter rope through one side of the double pulley. Thread the longer rope over the single pulley and then through the other wheel of the double pulley.

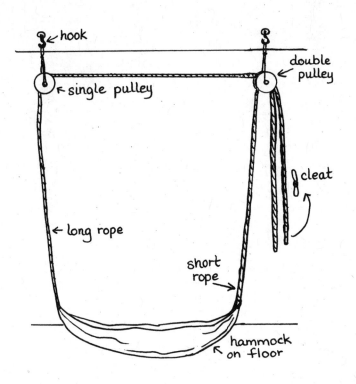

hook

single pulley

double pulley

cleat

long rope

short rope

hammock on floor

6. Show the children how to pull on both ropes at once to raise the hammock evenly and as high as they want it. Let them experiment with what happens if they pull only one rope, or if they pull one rope faster than the other. Show them how to wrap the rope in a figure eight around the cleat to keep the hammock in place.

Borrowing books from the library is free and environmentally friendly. You help save a tree, and if you walk you'll keep carbon dioxide from your car from entering the atmosphere.

GREEN IDEA · GREEN IDEA ·

# All Ages

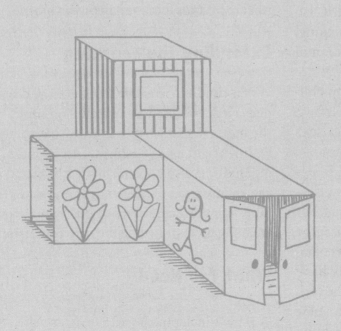

# Child-Safe Display Rack

## Who

All ages

## About the Toy

This display rack provides an easy, safe, and manageable way for children to display things and to change them when desired. The rack encourages independence and hand-eye coordination as the children hang and take down pictures at will. It also promotes language development, logical thinking, and sequencing skills when used for discussion of pictures or picture stories.

Use this display rack to dry or display children's artwork. Older children can hang their own pictures or pictures they have cut from magazines or calendars. They can also use the rack to arrange pictures in a sequence to tell a story about something they have done or learned about, or to classify and place pictures into like groups or pairs. For toddlers and young preschoolers, the rack can be used to display everyday objects and pictures of familiar people and places. During read-alouds, hang accompanying pictures or illustrations on the rack for children to use following the story in a fun new way. They will also enjoy seeing their artwork hung up to dry on the rack.

For infants, use the rack to hang within their line of sight large photographs and bright designs from magazines or posters. Infants are most interested in faces, colors, and design patterns. Should a slight breeze catch a photo and make it move, that would be a great source of interest for the baby.

## What They Learn

Approaches to learning development skills: Preschoolers and schoolagers are instinctively creative, and they enjoy original music, art, drama, and language. They are typically uncritical observers and, because of their age, have little perspective on artistic accomplishment. For example, they might believe a picture is finished simply because the paper is filled up. Arts-related activities that are developmentally appropriate and that incorporate movement, spontaneous expression, variety, and fun are best for four- and five-year-olds.

## Extending the Learning

When children's creative work is treated with care, displayed, and used as a discussion topic, it sends the message that what they create has value, which in turn heightens self-esteem. Display racks, including this one, also encourage preschool and school-age children to be independent and take responsibility for their artistic creations by ensuring they are hung up to dry when they are complete.

## What You Need

☐ 1-by-2-inch pine board

☐ sandpaper

□ spring-type clothespins (two per foot of board)

□ hammer and finishing nails

□ hand drill

□ pencil

□ ruler

□ wood glue

## How to Make It

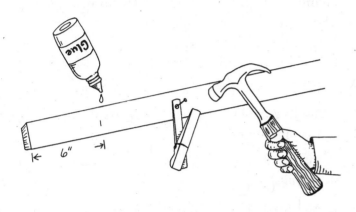

1. Cut the board to the desired length and sand it smooth. Measure and mark off 6-inch intervals along the board.

2. Twist clothespins apart slightly and drill a small hole about ½ to ¾ inch from the top of one half of the clothespin. (If clothespins should come apart, put them back together by snapping each half around the spring.)

3. Place a small dab of glue below the hole on the back of the clothespin. Place a clothespin at each designated mark.

4. Hammer a nail through each hole to attach clothespins to the board. Snap clothespin into place. Press to secure the glue.

*Note:* For a permanent display board, attach the rack firmly to the wall at the children's level. As an alternative, you can use it as a movable drying rack (for example, over a bathtub or laundry tub to dry doll clothes or between two chairs to hang mittens or special projects).

## Variation

For a quick and easy display system, attach half of a Velcro patch to the side of each clothespin. Stick the other half of the patch to a wall or a large board at the children's level. The clothespins will stick to the patches and can be used to hang items as discussed above. Located in a prominent place at an adult level, this variation also can be used to clip notes as reminders to staff, parents, or yourself.

Designate a box for scraps of construction paper. When children need a small piece of paper, they can use the paper in the box instead of cutting into a new sheet.

GREEN IDEA · GREEN IDEA

# Milk-Carton Puppets

## Who

All ages

## About the Toy

Puppets encourage children to tell stories, which develops language and memory skills. Often children who are shy about talking or who seem to forget what they want to say are comfortable expressing themselves through a puppet. Puppets also encourage children to create original stories. All of these skills contribute to reading readiness and literacy and help build self-esteem.

These puppets lend excitement to the telling of familiar stories and nursery rhymes. Bears, bunnies, kittens, puppies, and lambs are particularly useful puppets to have available.

## What They Learn

Language and communication development skills: Where does language come from? Although the experts continue to debate whether language

is preprogrammed or determined by input into specialized areas of the brain, it does appear that humans have a basic need to communicate. Even a child as young as two months who reaches out and points with one finger is practicing a form of language. Environments that help foster language development in infants include ones in which

- infants find adults' voices pleasant to listen to;
- adults respond positively to an infant's attempts to communicate;
- infants observe adults using language to communicate and solve problems;
- and adults share activities and talk about them with an infant, such as during daily routines, including while feeding the infant and changing her diapers.

In fact, environments such as these strengthen the language development of all young children, from toddlers through schoolagers.

## Extending the Learning

Puppets are important in early childhood classrooms and can add an exciting element to almost any story. Infants and toddlers will delight in seeing the puppets move and hearing the sounds they make. For toddlers and preschoolers, puppets are important because they invite children to imagine, involving them more intimately in the storytelling process. They will also enjoy using the puppets with fingerplays and rhymes. Older preschoolers and schoolagers can be encouraged to put on puppet shows for other children and family members, which will involve planning the puppet characters needed for the show and possibly constructing new ones.

## What You Need

### FOR EACH PUPPET:

☐ one clean paper milk carton

☐ pencil

☐ ruler

☐ scissors

☐ glue

☐ staples or needle and thread

☐ fabric and felt

☐ toilet paper roll

## How to Make It

### BUNNY

1. Cut off the top section of the milk carton. Choose a carton size that is most appropriate for the type of puppet and the hand size of the puppeteer. Thoroughly wash and dry the carton.

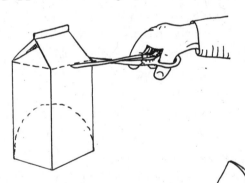

2. Place the carton on its bottom. Along one edge, make a mark 3 inches down from the top rim. On both sides, draw an arched line from the mark to the bottom corners. Cut along that line.

Trim away curved remnants, leaving a band around the top of the carton (which will be the bottom of the puppet).

3. Turn the carton over so the bottom side is up. Cut a square of felt (the color you want for the mouth) the size of the milk carton bottom and glue it on. Fold bottom diagonally and flip the curved section up to create the mouth and the face.

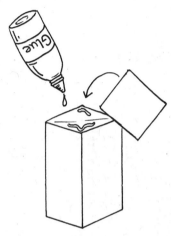

4. Cut the fabric to cover the carton and glue it on. For reinforcement, staple or sew around all edges. Sew small pieces of fabric to form arms and sew or staple them to the puppet body.

5. Cut ears from a toilet paper roll. Cut and glue felt to the inner ear and fur to the outer ear. Reinforce by sewing or stapling around each ear. Sew or staple the ears to the puppet head.

6. Cut black or other felt pieces for eyes and nose. Glue on the facial features and decorations.

## Variations

Using this pattern as your basic model, experiment with other materials and ideas to create puppets to suit your needs.

Reusing milk cartons to make puppets and other toys helps keep them out of landfills. Before you throw something away, ask yourself, "Can I use this again in a different way?" or "Can someone else use this?"

# Milk-Carton Blocks

## Who

All ages

## About the Toy

Block play helps children develop a wide range of skills. Because milk-carton blocks are so inexpensive, you can easily have enough for every child to play with, which is important for early social interaction and learning to work together.

## What They Learn

Cognitive development skills: Blocks have been a staple of early childhood classrooms for over a century—and for good reason. When young children play with blocks, they have opportunities to develop

- an understanding of basic concepts, such as balance, size, weight, height, and length;
- counting and categorizing skills;
- problem-solving skills;
- language skills and new vocabulary;

- social skills, such as cooperation and respect for others' space and building constructions;
- and small-muscle strength and coordination.

Changing or adding to the basic materials (unit blocks, hollow blocks) in a block center or area ensures children's continued engagement in the center and offers new opportunities for learning. Adding accessories to complement a particular unit of study, such as transportation or animals, is an easy and appropriate way to extend children's learning.

## Extending the Learning

Use these blocks with infants just learning to crawl to help with gross-motor development. For example, place small, colorful blocks just out of their reach, and encourage them to move toward the blocks. Let an infant sitting up handle and explore a small block. Most toddlers can stack between four to six blocks and then will often delight in knocking them down. They also will enjoy using the blocks for filling and dumping games. Preschoolers and schoolagers, who are at the perfect age for make-believe play involving blocks, will benefit from accessories such as toy people, animals, vehicles, and road signs. As they create pretend scenarios and elaborate constructions, watch and listen for signs of social development, such as the ability to work together toward a common goal, cooperate, share, and even compliment one another on a job well done.

## What You Need

FOR EACH BLOCK:

☐ two milk cartons or boxes of the same size
☐ scissors

- ☐ newspapers
- ☐ colorful contact or other durable paper
- ☐ tape or clear contact paper
- ☐ markers
- ☐ noise-making items

## How to Make It

1. Cut the top off each carton at the same place. (How much is cut off determines the height of the block.) Thoroughly wash and dry the cartons.

2. Slip one empty carton over the other to make a building block. For sturdier, weightier building blocks, stuff one of the bottoms with crumpled newspaper before fitting the second carton over it. (Be careful not to overstuff, which can round the sides and make building with them difficult.) If you're making a rhythm instrument, fill one carton with desired noise-making items (such as sand, pebbles, or rice) before fitting the second one over it.

3. Cover the block with colorful contact paper or wrap it like a package

with sturdy paper, such as a grocery bag, and tape the ends securely.

4. If desired, use markers to draw numbers or shapes on the block, or cut out decorations, place them on the block, and cover them with clear contact paper.

## Variations

Make dice for children to use with board games. Make a block with the height equal to the width, following the previous four steps. Cover the block with white paper and draw dots on it to resemble a die.

Make a shape sorter by cutting two cartons the same size (as previously described). Cover each of the open cartons with plain contact paper. Push cartons together. Draw shapes slightly larger than the objects intended to fit through the holes. With a utility knife, cut out the designs. These blocks will challenge children to take apart the two sections of the block and then match the correct shapes when they put them back together.

Make fit-together matching cubes. Follow the directions for making the die (see the first variation), using quart-, pint-, or cup-sized cartons. Create matching themes (number, pattern, or color) for each set of cubes. Apply half of a section of Velcro to two opposite sides of each cube, making sure that the hook and loop parts of the Velcro are attached in such a way that the child can match the cubes correctly.

This activity is a great way to reuse milk cartons. Ask for donations of milk cartons, and work with older children to make more blocks. They can give the blocks to younger children or take them home.

GREEN IDEA · GREEN IDEA

# Versatile Scoop Toy

## Who

All ages

## About the Toy

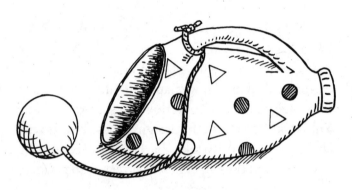

This scoop toy provides an example of using a discarded material in many fun and useful ways. The toy encourages infants to explore the characteristics of materials, whereas toddlers may use the scoop for imaginative play. The toy encourages older children to play together and create their own games.

## What They Learn

Approaches to learning development skills: Decisions about which types of toys and materials are appropriate for children of any age level should be based on three types of knowledge: age appropriateness, individual appropriateness, and cultural appropriateness. Age appropriateness involves how safe a toy is and whether the toy is interesting and challenging. Individual appropriateness involves knowledge of the strengths, interests, and needs of each child. Sometimes a toy or material must be modified to ensure it is safe and appropriate for a child or a group of children. Finally, cultural appropriateness involves taking into account the social and cultural contexts in which a child lives to ensure that learning experiences will be meaningful, relevant, and respectful of all children and their families.

## Extending the Learning

Some toys are appropriate for children of varying ages and abilities, even though they may play with the toy in very different ways. This scoop toy is an example of one such toy. Whereas an infant may simply examine the scoop and explore it with his hands, a toddler may put the scoop on his head as a helmet and march around the room with it on. Preschoolers and schoolagers are likely to use it to play catch using soft balls, such as pom-poms or whiffle balls.

## What You Need

- ☐ two or more empty laundry soap or bleach bottles
- ☐ scissors
- ☐ permanent markers
- ☐ light, soft ball

## How to Make It

1. Thoroughly wash and dry the bottles. Carefully cut each one to make a scoop. Yarn and glue or seam binding tape can be used to cover the cut edge of the scoop.

2. Use the permanent markers to decorate the scoop.

## Variation

For a ball and scoop game, braid a 2-foot length of yarn, tie one end to the scoop handle, and fasten a ball to the other end. The longer the string is, the harder the game will be. For younger or less skilled children, shorten the length of the yarn braid until they can work with it successfully.

**!** **CAUTION:** Do not leave string on the scoops if infants or very young toddlers will be using them.

Encourage recycling and reuse. Ask families to bring in clean, empty bleach or laundry soap bottles that you can use for additional scoops.

# Finger Puppets

## Who

All ages

## About the Toy

Puppets provide numerous learning experiences for children of all ages and can enhance a variety of everyday activities, such as read-alouds and dramatic play.

## What They Learn

Approaches to learning development skills: When first introducing puppets to children, try to give them access to many different kinds, such as hand puppets, finger puppets, paper-bag puppets, and puppets they make themselves, such as the Milk-Carton Puppets (see p. 202) from this book. Puppets can be used to help tell stories, and they can be used to help children learn about social behavior, including emotions, in nonthreatening ways. For example, it is often easier for children to discuss why a puppet is sad because her mom is out of town on business than it is for them to discuss why they might be sad.

## Extending the Learning

Through games such as peek-a-boo, puppets can help infants understand the concept of object permanence—that an object exists even when it is out of sight—as well as practice visual tracking and locating sounds. Toddlers will enjoy both imitating puppets' words and sounds and using the puppets to talk to one another or to you. Invite older toddlers, preschoolers, and schoolagers to wear the puppets to help tell or create stories. They may even want to create and perform their own puppet shows.

**!** **CAUTION:** Do not let infants or toddlers handle puppets that have small objects attached to them. If these objects come loose, they could be harmful.

## What You Need

- ☐ glove
- ☐ scissors
- ☐ needle and thread or fabric glue
- ☐ markers or fabric paint or bits of fabric, fringe, yarn, or ribbon
- ☐ container with lid

## How to Make It

1. Cut the fingers off the glove and hem or glue around the raw edge of each finger so it will not unravel.

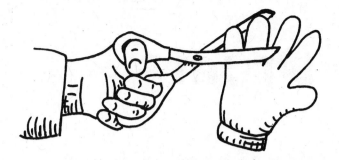

2. Sew, glue, or paint interesting faces onto the finger sections of each glove, adding fringe or other decorations for added interest.

This is great way to make use of gloves that have lost their mates.

# Bongo Drum

## Who

All ages

## About the Toy

Young children enjoy creating music, so always keep a variety of musical instruments (real and homemade) in the classroom.

## What They Learn

Approaches to learning development skills: Music brings joy and energy into early childhood classrooms, and it enhances children's learning in all developmental domains. Therefore, music should be a part of any early childhood program, and all children should be exposed to or participate in some type of music experience every day. A few of the benefits of music for young children include:

**Physical development:** Children develop muscular control, coordination, balance, and an awareness of body movement.

**Cognitive development:** Children develop perceptual skills, attention to detail, ability to focus, vocabulary, and comprehension skills.

**Social development:** Children develop the ability to participate, share, and cooperate.

**Emotional development:** Children develop self-confidence and the ability to clarify or identify their own feelings.

**Aesthetic development:** Children develop sensitivity to and an appreciation for many kinds of music.

## Extending the Learning

Infants and toddlers will enjoy hitting this drum and making noise, and the action of hitting helps them develop hand-eye coordination. Preschoolers and schoolagers can use the drum to keep time to or play along with recorded music, create their own rhythms, or use the drum in make-believe play. Beating the drums also enhances their upper body strength and coordination.

## What You Need

- ☐ metal can (such as a 2- or 3-pound coffee can)
- ☐ scissors
- ☐ colorful paper or contact paper
- ☐ crayons or markers
- ☐ glue
- ☐ clear contact paper
- ☐ plastic lid or piece of leather (up to 9 by 9 inches)

☐ string or heavy rubber band

☐ wooden spoon or dowel

## How to Make It

1. Cut a piece of paper to fit the outside of the can. Have children draw designs on the paper with crayons or markers.

2. Glue the paper to the can. For a longer lasting drum, place clear contact paper over the decorated paper, or simply cover the can with colorful contact paper.

3. Place the lid on the can. If you are using a piece of leather for the drum's top, cut a circle out of the leather a few inches wider than the rim of the can. Center the circle over the open end of the can. Wrap the string or rubber band several times around the can and the overlapping edges of the leather.

4. Use the wooden spoon or dowel for a drumstick. Make sure the spoon or dowel is smooth, splinter-free, and kidproof.

Consider starting a collection of homemade instruments (including the Banjo on p. 168), and encourage children to create their own classroom bands using only the homemade instruments.

GREEN IDEA • GREEN IDEA

# Crawl-Through Boxes and Tunnels

## Who

All ages

## About the Toy

These boxes are a fun toy for children of all ages.

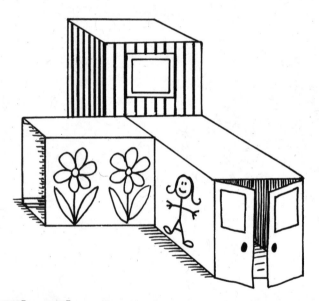

## What They Learn

Physical and motor development skills: The physical activities of children not only enhance their physical development but also contribute to cognitive and emotional growth. Therefore, it is important to provide all children with plenty of opportunities for physical movement each day. Most infants and toddlers respond positively to physical stimulation, such as bouncing and dancing to musical rhythms, climbing on structures, or crawling through tunnels. The physical play of preschoolers and schoolagers is more varied, since their gross- and fine-motor skills are more advanced. In addition, four- and five-year-olds have the cognitive ability to turn physical activities, such as crawling through box tunnels, into opportunities for make-believe play with other children and games involving rules.

## Extending the Learning

Use just one box for infants so they can practice crawling in a safe environment. Playing peek-a-boo with infants can help them work through separation anxiety. Talking about the process of crawling through the box and coming out the other end is reassuring to an infant and enhances her language development. Toddlers and preschoolers will need more of a challenge. Add boxes and create a maze of different turns and angles, and then encourage the children to try to catch one another as they scramble through the box tunnels. Invite schoolagers to design their own tunnels and mazes for games of chase or to use in make-believe play. Help extend their learning by inviting them to create mini versions of their mazes and tunnels in the block area using shoeboxes or blocks.

## What You Need

☐ sturdy cardboard boxes

☐ extra cardboard for reinforcing strips

☐ pencil

☐ ruler

☐ utility knife or box cutter

☐ glue or tape

☐ carpet squares, or fuzzy or smooth fabric pieces

## How to Make It

**FOR EACH BOX:**

1. Cut four pieces of cardboard 5 inches wide and the length of the box. Measure and score each piece 1 inch in from the edge of the long sides.

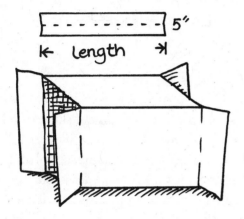

2. Open both ends of each box. Bend the scored parts slightly. Apply glue to the outside of the bent parts. Glue each piece into the inside corners of the box, forming a triangular brace. When dry, reinforce with tape.

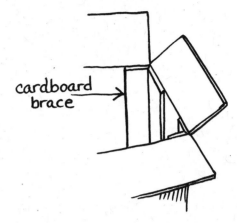

cardboard brace

3. Glue materials and fabrics to the inside of the box. If desired, cover the outside of the box with fabric scraps.

4. To make tunnels and mazes, reinforce as in steps 1 and 2. Add textures or decorations to fit the theme, and tape the boxes together.

Contact local appliance stores for donations of large boxes.

# Step-Up Aerobics

## Who

All ages

## About the Toy

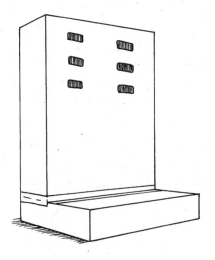

The step-up encourages children to exercise the muscles in their legs. It introduces them to the notion that using their legs not only builds strong leg muscles but also is an important part of overall aerobic health because it benefits their lungs and heart. The step-up also helps children learn the concept of *left* and *right,* practice counting, and experience the joy of using their bodies.

Add this piece of inexpensive workout equipment to the large-muscle area for children to use as they like or as part of a group exercise activity. Infants and young toddlers can explore the use of their bodies by either climbing or stepping on the step-up. Older toddlers and younger preschoolers can practice stepping up and down.

Older preschoolers and schoolagers may be encouraged to count as they step up and down or to practice their understanding of *right* and *left* by saying, "right foot up; right foot down; left foot up; left foot down." Use the step-up with music.

You can make the step-up wide enough so several children can use it side by side, or you can make it four-sided for group aerobic exercise. Discuss with the children how walking, running, and using the step-up helps keep their hearts healthy and strong.

## What They Learn

Physical and motor development skills: The National Association for Sport and Physical Education (NASPE) recommends that preschool and school-age children accumulate *at least* 60 minutes of moderate to vigorous physical activity most days of the week. This does not mean, however, that the activity must be sustained over a 60-minute period. In fact, given the developmental levels of children this age, both physically and mentally, it would be difficult for them to do so. At this age, children's physical activities consist of short bursts of energy or short games and activities such as chase, hopscotch, climbing, running, and riding toy vehicles or bicycles. Most important, physical activities for preschoolers and schoolagers should be developmentally appropriate, varied, and fun.

## Extending the Learning

Children who participate in and enjoy physical activities at a young age are more likely to make physical activity a regular part of their lifestyles as adults. When participating in physical activities with children, be sure to convey a positive and energetic attitude—your enthusiasm can greatly affect the way children view physical activities too.

This piece of inexpensive workout equipment can be used by infants and toddlers as well as older children. Younger children will practice gross-motor skills when they climb and step on the step-up boxes. Two- and three-year-olds can use the step-up to practice stepping skills. Older preschoolers and schoolagers can be encouraged to create their own step-aerobic routines by counting their steps and indicating whether to step up with their right or left foot. Consider playing CDs while the children exercise, and challenge them to step up and down to the beat of the music.

## What You Need

- [ ] two sturdy cardboard boxes
- [ ] newspapers
- [ ] duct tape
- [ ] utility knife

## How to Make It

1. For the base, stuff crumpled newspaper into a flat cardboard box that is approximately 8 by 18 by 18 inches. Box sizes will vary according to the size of children using the step-up and whether or not it is intended for use by a single child or multiple children. Securely tape the openings shut.

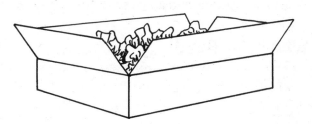

2. For the handle box, choose a tall, sturdy box that, when placed on end, is approximately 10 by 18 inches and tall enough for the tallest child in the group to hold onto comfortably. Open up one end of the box, and tape all other sides shut.

3. Lay the base box in a horizontal position. Place the tall box with the open end up, aligning one side of the tall box with the back of the base. Tape the two boxes securely together. Push the flaps of the open end inside the box for reinforcement. Cut the small openings (handles) at appropriate height for shorter children.

4. Cover both boxes with contact paper or let children decorate them with markers.

## Variation

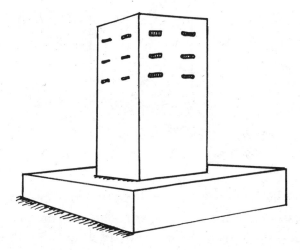

For a four-sided step-up, choose a large enough base box to allow about 8 inches on all four sides when the handle box is placed in the middle. Proceed as for the single-person step-up.

Are there places you normally drive to that you could walk or ride a bike to instead? Walking and biking are totally green methods of transportation, and they are great ways to exercise.

GREEN IDEA · GREEN IDEA

# Bug Keeper

## Who

All ages

## About the Toy

Use this bug keeper to store insects and plants that preschoolers and schoolagers collect. Children can study the insects for a day or two, and then let them go. The bug collector provides the hands-on, concrete experience that makes the use of other resources—such as books and discussions—a richer, more meaningful learning experience for all children.

## What They Learn

Approaches to learning development skills: Young children learn science concepts through discovery, exploration, and experiences that build on their prior knowledge. By exploring and experimenting with their environment, children acquire the scientific thinking skills of problem-solving and forming concepts. Introductions to plants, animals, and insects at an early age enables children to cultivate an understanding of and respect for other living things.

## Extending the Learning

This bug keeper can be used for children ages two to five. It enables toddlers and young preschoolers to examine insects—things in the environment they sometimes fear—from a safe distance. Encourage two- and three-year-olds to look closely at the insects and notice features such as number of legs, type of eyes, and color and design of body. Older children can collect plants and insects from outside and observe them over several days before releasing them. Help four- and five-year-olds learn more about the plants and insects that interest them by reading about them or watching nature videos. Provide children with paper and drawing tools, and invite them to create their own bug books based on their observations and any information they learn.

## What You Need

☐ wide-mouth clear plastic jar with lid
☐ scissors
☐ clean stocking or panty hose
☐ two twist ties from bread bags, or rubber bands

## How to Make It

1. Cut two or three windows out of the sides of the jar.

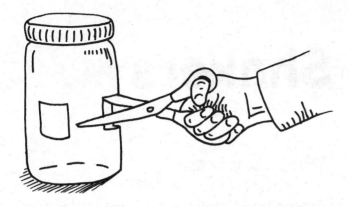

2. Slip the jar into a leg of the stocking (the lighter the color and the finer the knit, the better). Cut off the foot and upper part of the stocking, leaving 6 inches at each end.

3. Gather the stocking to one side of the jar's bottom and fasten it with a twist tie or rubber band. Gather insects and plants. Place the insects in the jar and cover with the lid. Fasten the top of the stocking with another twist tie or rubber band.

Return the bugs to their natural habitat after the children have observed them. Talk with the children about habitat protection.

GREEN IDEA · GREEN IDEA

# Rhythm Shakers

## Who

All ages

## About the Toy

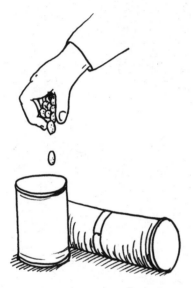

Depending on their age, children will find their own unique ways of using the rhythm shakers. Make a variety of shakers with different sounds for infants and toddlers to experiment with. To provide additional sensory experiences, consider covering the shakers with bright materials or materials with different textures. Provide older children with these same types of materials and invite them to decorate the shakers any way they wish. They can also create chants or shaker songs to perform for other children.

## What They Learn

Approaches to learning development skills: Infants and toddlers are in the process of learning about cause and effect—that they can act upon their environment and make things happen. That is why toys that make noise or move certain ways when infants manipulate them are so fascinating. These types of toys also encourage them to practice gross-motor skills, such as waving, shaking, pushing, or pulling. For older children, the shakers encourage music-making, rhythm, and creative expression. Older children can also experiment with cause and effect by making a variety of shakers to learn how different amounts of noise-making materials change the sounds the shakers produce.

## Extending the Learning

As the children use the shakers, see if they naturally try new ways to move them. If needed, encourage the children to move the shakers to create quiet sounds and loud sounds. Are the children aware of the differences?

## What You Need

☐ metal or plastic container and cover

☐ noise-making materials (such as buttons, small bells tied together with sturdy thread, dried beans, rice, popcorn, or pebbles)

☐ tape

# How to Make It

1. Put a small amount of noise-making material into the container.

2. Tape the cover securely in place.

Be sure to add the shakers to the permanent collection of classroom instruments for children to experiment with. Encourage the children to use them to produce fun sound effects during read-alouds.

GREEN IDEA · GREEN IDEA

# Reusable and Donated Materials Index